西北民居第一宅

The No. 1 of the
Domestic Architecture in
Northwestern China

姜氏庄园

Jiang

Family

Manor

米脂县姜氏庄园文物管理所　编著

艾克生　主编

文物出版社

图书在版编目（CIP）数据

姜氏庄园 / 米脂县姜氏庄园文物管理所编著 ; 艾克生
主编 . — 北京 : 文物出版社 , 2016.6
ISBN 978-7-5010-4633-1

Ⅰ . ①姜… Ⅱ . ①米… ②艾… Ⅲ . ①古建筑遗址 —
介绍 — 米脂县 — 清代 Ⅳ . ① K878.3

中国版本图书馆 CIP 数据核字（2016）第 135053 号

姜氏庄园

编　　著：米脂县姜氏庄园文物管理所
主　　编：艾克生

封面题字：刘文西
责任编辑：戴　茜
装帧设计：特木热
责任印制：梁秋卉

出版发行：文物出版社
社　　址：北京市东直门内北小街 2 号楼
邮　　编：100007
网　　址：http://www.wenwu.com
邮　　箱：web@wenwu.com
经　　销：新华书店
印　　刷：北京鹏润伟业印刷有限公司
开　　本：889mm×1194mm　1/12
印　　张：16
版　　次：2016 年 6 月第 1 版
印　　次：2016 年 6 月第 1 次印刷
书　　号：ISBN 978-7-5010-4633-1
定　　价：280.00 元

姜氏莊園

Jiang Family Manor

008 陕北窑洞民居的瑰宝（序一）/ 王军

Preface I

The Treasure of the Cave Dwelling-style

Domestic Architecture in Northern Shaanxi

012 窑洞院落的经典之作——姜氏庄园（序二）/ 郭冰庐

Preface II

A Masterpiece of the Cave Courtyard Architecture

——the Jiang Family Manor

018 一位文物工作者的艰辛与追求

　　　——写在《姜氏庄园》画册付梓之际 / 乔建军

The Hardships and Pursuits of a Cultural Heritage Conserver

—— at the Publishing of the Album *Jiang Family Manor*

概述 026
Brief Introduction

历史沿革 030
The History and Development of
the Jiang Family Manor

创业发家 034
The Starting and Flourishing
of the Family

庄园建造 038
The Construction
of the Manor

建筑特点 040
The Characteristics
of the Architectural Complex

西北民居第一宅 050
——姜氏庄园（解说词）
The Jiang Family Manor
—— The No. 1 of the Domestic Architecture in Northwestern China

后记 188
Postscript

序一

陕北窑洞民居的瑰宝

王军

　　由米脂县姜氏庄园文物管理所编纂的《姜氏庄园》画册蓝本面世，有幸先睹为快。在当今快节奏的时代，图片更易直观地给人们带来视觉冲击。打开这本画册，犹如一轴长长的画卷渐次呈现——一幅幅精美的图片，一段段翔实的文字，仿佛将人带入陕北文化的广阔境地，从而对这片神奇的土地充满遐想。画册从各个层面、不同角度，展示着姜氏庄园的历史价值与文化魅力，使黄土地上的这颗璀璨的民居瑰宝放射出夺目的光彩。看着这些精美的图片也使我心潮澎湃，思绪万千。

　　早在 30 年前，我就与姜氏庄园结下了不解之缘。1985 年夏，我与我的老师侯继尧教授初次来到姜氏庄园，就被庄园的神奇设计和精湛工艺所震惊。面对黄土高坡上长出的窑洞民居奇葩，作为建筑学专业的教师，对前辈设计者及建造工匠们的敬佩之情油然而生。我们心怀敬畏地对这座窑洞经典进行了初步测绘，首次为姜氏庄园绘制了平、立、剖面图，对其空间艺术和建造技术做了初步研究，这些成果都在 1989 年侯继尧教授编著的《窑洞民居》及 1999 年侯继尧教授与我合著的《中国窑洞》中展示给了读者。

　　2000 年，北京中华民族博物院要建 56 个民族的代表性民居，将姜氏庄园选作汉族民居建筑的代表，其施工图设计由侯教授与我承担。为此，我带领研究生住在刘家峁村，对姜氏庄园再次进行了为期 12 天的详细测绘，并用电脑绘制了庄园的准确测绘图，这些成果在我 2009 年出版的专著《西北民居》中奉献给了读者。与此同时，我也多次在国外学术交流中自豪地把姜氏庄园介绍给了海外的学者们。

　　姜氏庄园不仅是一部古朴瑰丽的古建筑典籍，更是黄土风情浓郁的史诗。它以深厚的人文内涵及独特的地域风采，堪称"西北民居第一宅"。它所承载的营建智慧，至今仍是地域建筑创作的源泉，而以窑洞群构筑的姜氏庄园也是今天人们追求的绿色建筑的典范。

　　窑洞是生活在黄河中上游地区的人们最传统、最典型的民居建筑形式。它最早源自原始先民的穴居文化，经过几千年的沧桑变迁，窑洞从内容到形式不断发展，呈现出鲜明的地域特色和独特的民居建筑风格。而陕北窑洞，则以其恢宏大气、粗犷豪迈为灵魂。

　　纵观姜氏庄园，在恢宏大气的烘托下，又展示出清灵俊秀的细部。其背靠峰峦，面向溪水，依山而建，三层院落依次递进，设计巧妙，布局严谨，拱洞相连，

Preface I

The Treasure of the Cave Dwelling-style Domestic Architecture in Northern Shaanxi

Wang Jun

I am lucky to read the sketch of the album titled *Jiang Family Manor* compiled by the Commission for Preservation of the Jiang Family Manor in Mizhi County before it is published. Reading this album, just like unrolling a painting scroll, I feel like being brought into the vast landscape of the northern Shaanxi culture by the beautiful pictures and terse but clear captions, and indulged into the fanciful imaginations. From various scenarios and angles, this album displays the historic values and cultural charm of the Jiang Family Manor and releases the dazzling luster of this rare jewel of domestic architecture on the Loess Plateau.

Cave dwelling is the most traditional and typical domestic architectural type in the upper and middle reaches of the Yellow River, and the soul of the cave dwellings of the northern Shaanxi is the magnificent style and plain and generous spirit.

Generally seen, the Jiang Family Manor shows a magnificent and plain style; however, it also has many elaborate and elegant details. Backing against the mountain and facing the creek, it is built as a three-storied courtyard complex in clever design and compact planning. Meandering in the courtyards, we can see the carriers of the traditional cultures everywhere: the brick carvings, stone sculptures, wood carvings and color paintworks and other artistic languages reflect the aesthetic ideas and value concepts of the people in this area.

The unusualness of the Jiang Family Manor is also favored from Mizhi County, where it is located. The special geographic environment and profound resources of culture and humanities granted this cave manor a unique individuality and temperament. Meanwhile, Mizhi is also a cultural center of the northern Shaanxi and a county with plenty of historic and cultural heritages in Shaanxi Province.

The publishing of the album *Jiang Family Manor* by the Cultural Relics Press is a gratifying event, which reflects its splendid past and shows its future. It is also clearly seen that Mr. Ai Kesheng, the director of

曲径通幽。漫步庭院，随处可见传统文化的载体，砖雕石刻、木雕彩绘等艺术化的语言，表达着一方人士的审美理念与价值观念，可谓"求工于一笔之内，寄情于点画之间"。在建筑主体及局部设置上，无不蕴含期盼平安吉祥、耕读传家、风水理念的传统道德风范。姜氏庄园集窑洞民居建筑之大成，是研究窑洞文化及窑洞衍生的非物质文化的生动教材，是中华窑洞民居建筑文化的瑰宝。

姜氏庄园的神奇，也得益于所在地米脂县，特殊的区位环境和丰厚的地气人脉，赋予了窑洞庄园独有的个性和气质。米脂，因沃壤宜粟，"米汁淅之如脂"而得名，是一处有着悠久历史和灿烂文化并曾为中国人民的解放事业做出过特殊贡献的地方。米脂，钟灵毓秀，人才辈出，闯王故里，貂蝉家乡，这里的水土养育了无数杰出的英雄儿女。翻开史册，那一个个耳熟能详的名字令人敬仰，让人赞叹！

米脂，是陕北文化之乡，是陕西文物大县。在这里有历史上形成的盘龙山古建筑群，还有杨家沟骥村古寨、刘家峁姜氏庄园、高庙山常氏庄园，以及诸多的寺庙、石窟等古建筑文化景观。而米脂的窑洞文化又在中国建筑史上留下了浓浓墨迹。

《姜氏庄园》画册由文物出版社出版发行，令人深感欣慰，既彰显其辉煌的过去，也昭示着未来，不难看出艾克生所长付出了艰辛的努力。十年磨一剑，潜心攻文史，镜头审视庄园情，光影定格窑洞魂。他博采众长，竭心尽力，与同仁携手，这些文字和影像结集成册，更将扩大姜氏庄园在海内外的影响力，也为当今乡土建筑设计提供了翔实的参考资料。

《姜氏庄园》画册带着墨香奉献给读者，它所表现和承载的内容博大而精深，必将对米脂文化旅游事业的发展与繁荣产生巨大的推动作用。编者怀着热爱家乡、勤勉敬业的热诚，以求真务实的态度和认真负责的精神，力图保持人文历史的真实，使画册具有较强的史实性、研究性和观赏性，给人们留下了一份珍贵的文化遗产。

勉作数言，聊以为序。

2015 年 12 月　于西安

王军 / Wang Jun

西安建筑科技大学教授、博士生导师，国家级重点学科"建筑设计及其理论"学科带头人之一，中国民族建筑研究会民居建筑专业委员会副主任委员，中国建筑学会生土建筑分会副理事长，中国城市规划学会城市生态规划建设学术委员会委员，中国城市科学研究会绿色建筑与节能专业委员会委员。

the Commission for Preservation of the Jiang Family Manor, has spent hard work for this album. He accepted all of the favorable suggestions and did his best to compile the pictorial and textural materials into this book with his colleagues, the work of whom will increase the influence of the Jiang Family Manor at home and in abroad, and also provided reliable references for the designing of the contemporary vernacular architecture.

I hope this hastily composed short article can be a suitable preface.

December 2015, in Xi'an

序二

窑洞院落的经典之作——姜氏庄园

郭冰庐

恢宏大气的姜氏庄园，布局严谨的姜氏庄园，备极工巧的姜氏庄园，无论从哪一个角度看，姜氏庄园都是中华大地上窑洞院落的经典之作。

姜氏庄园是一座典型的石拱窑洞四合院聚落组合，也就是说，它属于地下掩土建筑石拱窑洞群，但又是以四合院形式布局。这不由让人联想到北京的砖木结构四合院和有"小北京"之称的榆林四合院。据说，姜氏庄园是由主人姜耀祖专请北京土木建筑专家设计，又请本地手艺高强的泥瓦匠、石匠、木匠、画匠等通力合作而完成的。至于是从北京学来的，还是参考杨家沟马氏庄园窑洞四合院，抑或是就近仿自榆林城四合院，不得而知。但这种窑洞四合院确实是砖木结构四合院在窑洞聚落中的一大发展，创意独特。

严谨的院落布局。姜氏庄园以中庭大门—月洞门—垂花门—圆门转扇—主庭正窑中孔为中轴线，由主庭（上院）、中庭（中院）、铺子院（下院）、左右两暗院（上院厨房院、库房院）、碾磨院（中院西侧）、葡萄院（中院东侧）共大小 7 座院落和寨墙、涵洞、井楼、窨子等设施组成。这种布局设计极为精妙，对于一座院落来说，不仅功能齐全，还充分利用了体量空间，从方位布局和立体等差上使聚落次第变化、错落有致，又对主庭起到了烘托、缓冲和保护的作用。

"明五暗四六厢窑"形制的代表作。"明五暗四六厢窑"是陕北经典窑洞院落的固定模式。姜氏庄园严格按照"明五暗四六厢窑"的规矩布局主庭，并以此为基准设计整个宅院。主庭宽 18.7、进深 22.05 米，中庭宽 14.85、进深 15.6 米，东西两暗院各两孔，东西厢窑各三孔，形成窑洞四合院"明五暗四六厢窑"的标准制式。如此安排，最大的特点是严谨而富于变化，保证了各窑纳阳、采光、通风充分，出路方便。中庭东西各三间大厢房。所特异者，东厢房较西厢房高 0.2 米，盖遵古代东为上、为青龙的"昭穆之制"。主庭东西厢窑之后，各箍进深 14 米的"枕头窑"，体量特别大，是为仓窑，因是储藏之所在，巧妙地隐匿于东西两厢窑之后，外人不经意是很难发现的。

涵洞和寨墙——周全的防卫体系。涵洞和寨墙是姜氏庄园一组和谐统一的交通与防卫体系。第一道寨墙斩土块石镶砌，高 9.5 米，上筑女儿墙和炮台，巡

Preface II

A Masterpiece of the Cave Courtyard Architecture — the Jiang Family Manor

Guo Binglu

The Jiang Family Manor is a typical stone vault cave quadrangle courtyard complex, which means that it belongs to a subterranean architecture — stone vault cave dwelling group, but has the plan of a courtyard complex. This form brings the brick-and-timber structure *siheyuan* courtyards in Beijing and the quadrangle courtyards which were called as "Micro-Beijing" in Yulin. It is said that this manor was designed by the architects invited by its owner, Jiang Yaozu, and built by the skilled and famous bricklayers, masons, carpenters and painters employed locally in their cooperative efforts. This cave quadrangle courtyard form is indeed a great development of the brick-and-timber structure *siheyuan* courtyard form in the cave dwelling type with innovative ideas.

Mr. Ai Kesheng, the director of the Commission for Preservation of the Jiang Family Manor, showed me the proof copy of the album *Jiang Family Manor* to review and asked me for a preface; I willingly agreed, because I know that the Jiang Family Manor is indeed a masterpiece of the cave-style domestic architecture of our county. As a rare cultural heritage, it has rich connotations for us to discover and inherit. The Jiang

此南行右拐进第二道涵洞，出洞则至额题"武魁"的中庭大门（正门）。对面则为高 8、长 10 余米的第二道寨墙和可上寨顶的额题"保障"的第三道涵洞。头道寨墙东端有井楼，设辘轳、水仓和控扼沟底要冲之瞭望孔。碾磨院西侧一土窑内有"跑贼"窨子通后山。中庭又较铺子院高 5 米，以暗道相连，供内部交通和传递信息之用，极其隐蔽却又相当便捷。两座 9 米以上的寨墙、三条寨门涵洞、两座大门，加上井楼、窨子的有机组合和恰当分割，是交通、闭藏、防卫、供水、泄洪五者的有力保证，说"固若金汤"不为过分。

别出心裁的"保障"设施。额题"保障"的第二道寨墙高于宅院一倍以上，石砌的寨墙面对大门，不是对外而是对内，被戏之为"反穿皮袄"。这是因为第一道入口的"大岳屏藩"寨墙是保卫宅院，具有防御功能，此第二道"保障"寨墙则起到"逃离"和"反攻"的双重功能。一旦各院失陷，则人畜细软可穿"保障"寨门涵洞顺利转移后山。届时寨门一关，守此寨头，居高临下，整个院落尽在掌控之中，是一种防卫—退却—反攻—收复环环相扣的防卫体系。

生态环保的交通兼具泄洪体系。诚然，这是一座石头造就的寨堡。如前所述，自沟底盘旋而上的明坡和三处寨门斜坡涵洞，中间均为片石竖插的宽 1.6 米的车马道，两侧又分别铺有宽 0.9 米的青石台阶，是

为人行道，此与当今之都市中为车行道、侧为人行道、人车分流的大马路别无二致。而庄园建于清代，其独特创意令人叹为观止！巧妙之处还在于，无论是涵洞，还是陡坡，均做成两边高中间低的凹形。如此设计，即使是大雨瓢泼、山洪倾泻，雨水亦可沿石坡直泻沟底，不带泥沙，纯净至极。从沟底仰望，波光粼粼，宛若蛟龙吐蕊，成为一道独特的风景。姜氏庄园从来没有发生过斜溜、塌方、泥石流等次生灾害，具有生态环保的意义。

坐便器——超前的生活设施。在姜氏庄园主庭的西南角设有专供净手的厕窑。厕窑内厕所设一坐便器。坐便器呈椅子状，中挖一孔，酷似今天的抽水马桶，后有靠背，侧旁有挡板扶手。这在清代同治、光绪年间绝对是一种创造，而其迄今已经正常使用了百余年，也确是一个奇迹。

造型艺术的审美情趣。"建筑是凝固的音乐，音乐是流动的建筑。"作为地下空间生土建筑类型的窑洞，在建筑构图上遵循"减法法则"，其建筑形象与一般建筑大异其趣。它以其自身特有的艺术风格体现了窑居者和民间工匠的审美追求。窑洞建筑的载体是院落，其"田园风光"情趣是要在苍凉和壮阔的背景中装点江山，化呆板单调为神奇。姜氏庄园窑洞群坐落在名曰牛家梁山的凹窝处，沿精细铺就的石坡而上，左拐钻过镌刻"大岳屏藩"寨门涵洞，额题"大夫第"

Family Manor has become a key tourist hotspot in Mizhi County even the entire northern Shaanxi: it attracts the students of the fine art academies and schools to come to practice drawing and painting, photographers to take pictures and experts and scholars to survey and study in various angles and aspects. As the director of director of the Commission for Preservation of the Jiang Family Manor, Mr. Ai Kesheng and his colleagues stay with this rare pearl of the domestic architecture, spare no efforts on seeking and trimming materials to mine the cultural connotations from them. Because of these reasons mentioned above, I am glad to write this preface for this album.

December 10, 2015

的前庭及汲水兼炮楼的井窑便赫然在目。再折回来穿过曲尺形的第二道涵洞，始见额题"武魁"斗拱举架的中庭大门。过月洞门是豁然开朗的中庭大院，再拾级而上，入垂花门，为恢宏大气的主庭。其运用对称轴线和主景轴线的转换推移，将"步异景移"、"峰回路转"的构图手法发挥得淋漓尽致。窑洞造型的最大特点是在"中矩"即方形院落的背景下以弧形的拱壳"中规"造型，均衡统一，比例适度，以富有韵律感而形成观赏序列。无论从室内的窑顶或室外的拱头线来看，无不以"圆美"架构之。如此，"中规"与"中矩"相济，不但使聚落富有变化，而且体现了中华民族传统的对大自然"天圆地方"的认识观念。姜氏庄园正是在这种"天圆地方"的认知理念上架构其美学理想的。

米脂县姜氏庄园文物管理所艾克生所长持来《姜氏庄园》画册清样给我看，并请我为画册写序，我欣然领命。原因是，姜氏庄园确实是我国窑洞民居的经典之作。作为一份宝贵的文化遗产，其内涵之丰富，值得我们去挖掘，去继承。姜氏庄园已经成为米脂乃至陕北旅游的重点项目，美术院校学生来此写生，摄影艺术家来此拍照，专家学者从不同的角度对其考察研究。2015 年 7 月 15 日，中国民协及陕西省文联、民协组织的"中国窑洞文化遗产田野考察陕北行"在中国民协党组书记罗杨同志的带领下，对姜氏庄园及其他陕北窑洞民居进行了现场考察，使对姜氏庄园的田野考察进入到一个新的阶段。人民日报记者马德州以《窑洞文化寻踪》为题做了报道；白旭旻、李向红、陈子矞以《陕北窑洞：中国文化遗产的又一活化石》为题的深度报道发表在 2015 年 8 月 14 日的《陕西日报》上。而作为姜氏庄园文物管理所所长的艾克生先生，自文管所成立之始，就与全所同仁在艰苦的条件下，守望着这一民居瑰宝，不遗余力地搜求资料，整理研究，挖掘其文化内涵。在这一过程中艾克生先生也成了研究姜氏庄园的专家。基于以上原因，本人欣然命笔，为之序。

2015 年 12 月 10 日

郭冰庐 / Guo Binglu

陕西洛川县人。榆林学院教授，陕北民间文化研究专家，其窑洞文化专著《窑洞风俗文化》获由中国文学艺术界联合会、中国民间文艺家协会共同颁发的"山花奖"（2004 ～ 2006）三等奖。

一位文物工作者的艰辛与追求

——写在《姜氏庄园》画册付梓之际

乔建军

由于工作的关系，我与米脂县姜氏庄园文物管理所艾克生所长非常熟悉。

姜氏庄园位于米脂县城东刘家峁村，是清末民初闻名陕北的大财主姜耀祖的一处宅院，建于清同治、光绪年间（1871～1886 年），堪称陕北窑洞民居建筑的艺术典范。时间更迭，人事变迁，庄园历经百余年虽未修葺，但整体建筑尚属完好。2001 年，米脂县政府克服重重困难，成立了"米脂县姜氏庄园文物管理所"，这为姜氏庄园在新的历史时期再放异彩奠定了基础。

2003 年，艾克生被调任姜氏庄园文物管理所所长。这位从 16 岁参加工作且在文化系统供职长达 40 余年的中年男子，早先就有写作经历。他写过不少剧本，分别被搬上舞台，有的剧目曾参加过省市文艺会演，多次获创作奖励，一些作品在国家、省、市戏剧评选中入围、获奖，并曾在多家报纸杂志上刊登和发表。他先后调入米脂县博物馆、文物公安特派室，至姜氏庄园文物管理所成立之时已有十余年文博工作经验。出任所长的那一年，他的工作状态是名副其

实的"一人一马一杆枪"。这一年，他只能在主管部门米脂县文化局办公并开展业务、翻阅文献、找寻资料。遗憾的是，如此一处辉煌的建筑，有关庄园与主人姜耀祖的故事传遍城乡，可相关文献对庄园却毫无记载，无任何可寻的资料，一切都得从零开始。然而，当时最大的困难，还要算庄园征购一事。堂堂姜氏大院，单位牌子已经挂起，竟无办公之所。因此，他一面配合协调征购工作，一面为开馆做必要的准备。

2004 年 4 月 28 日，他带领 5 名工作人员入驻姜氏庄园，对征购回来的房屋进行手续接交、清理和管护。历史问题，错综复杂，他也深知，既然接管工作不能一次性解决，那就因地制宜，从点滴做起。对他来说，有了单位，有了人员，自然也就有了压力，关键是如何尽快让人们知道姜氏庄园的存在。经过短时间的筹备之后，5 月 1 日，姜氏庄园正式对外开放，这是姜氏庄园沉寂多年后首次面向社会，由传统建筑上升为文物古迹，由民居院落转变为旅游景点。由私人居住过渡到政府管理，这为加强姜氏庄园的文

The Hardships and Pursuits of a Cultural Heritage Conserver

—at the Publishing of the Album *Jiang Family Manor*

Qiao Jianjun

The Jiang Family Manor located at Liujiamao Village to the east of Mizhi County seat is the residence of Jiang Yaozu, a famous rich landlord in the late Qing Dynasty and early Minguo Period. It is built in the Tongzhi and Guangxu Eras of the Qing Dynasty (1871-1886), and can be regarded as the model of the cave dwelling-style domestic architecture art of the northern Shaanxi.

In 2003, Mr. Ai Kesheng was assigned as the director of the Commission for Preservation of the Jiang Family Manor. In the over a decade since then, he worked under hard conditions with his colleagues, and they not only fulfilled the tasks of acquisition and rescue maintenance of the Jiang Family Manor, but also increased the publicizing and the promoting its popularity, and complied and composed the files about the history of the manor and the background of the Jiang Family based on the archives and historic literature and the results of their onsite investigations.

Mr. Ai Kesheng has strong devotion to his duty and never spare efforts from the professional training, and also has good achievements on the studies of ancient architecture and folklore. His original views and understandings to the historic and cultural connotations carried by the Jiang Family Manor, especially the caption written by him, are widely praised and highly approved by the experts and professional insiders.

The best pleasure in the human life is creating while contributing, which is also true to Kesheng. During the past decade, he dedicated himself to the academic studies and looked down upon the fame and wealth. He holds on in the Jiang Family Manor, a small universe for him, the happiness and sadness in it would never be known by the others.

Jiang Family Manor being published is the first illustrated comprehensive introduction of the

物保护工作并逐步对其进行开发，创造了有利条件。

　　姜氏庄园文物管理所地处农村，交通不便，环境较差，面对诸多困难，工作人员迎难而上，创造性地开展工作。深入民间，身背照相机，骑上摩托车，跑坟茔，抄碑文，阅族谱，尽量还原历史真实，力争把僵滞的历史遗迹，变为鲜活的人文形态，这是克生所长及其同仁们刻意追求和开发打造姜氏庄园的基本思路。经过数月，整理撰写出了有关姜氏庄园人文历史和家族背景的第一手资料。

　　2007年，克生所长多方筹措资金，对存在严重安全隐患的寨墙、厢房和门楼等建筑进行了抢救性维修，2009年，新建了停车场，2015年，对西南寨墙进行了抢救性维修，旅游环境得到进一步改善。

　　多年来，克生所长和其他工作人员努力加大宣传力度，力争让更多的人了解姜氏庄园。中央电视台《东方时空·直播时刻》栏目组曾在这里面向全球做了现场直播报道；此后，央视《走遍中国》和《欢乐中国行》、陕西电视台国际部《影像》和《资讯宽带网》及榆林电视台《文化长廊》栏目等，又分别在这里录制了多期节目；影视剧《刘志丹与谢子长》、《延安颂》、《张思德》、《血色浪漫》、《日出日落》、《西安事变》、《知青》、《向日葵》、《延安爱情》和《盘龙卧虎高山顶》等十余部剧目在这里选景拍摄。姜氏庄园的影响力和知名度日益提高。

　　克生所长是个事业心很强的人。在繁忙的工作中，他没有放松自己的业务学习。凡是他不掌握的知识，不是找张，就去问李，直到弄明白为止。一位职工感慨地说："一个月30天，咱领导就上班29天。"这句朴实的话语，充分表现出了克生所长对待工作一丝不苟、守职尽责的精神。最让他欣慰的是，中央候补委员、国家计生委主任、原陕西省委副书记王侠参观姜氏庄园时，对他出色的讲解高度赞赏，赠送他毛主席像章一枚。这份珍贵的礼品，是对他工作能力和态度的肯定，更是对他今后继续努力、奋进不息的精神鼓励。记得有一次，我陪同省市业务部门领导前往姜氏庄园参观调研时，克生所长亲自为客人讲解，热情的态度，生动的语言，引来阵阵掌声和笑声。

　　克生所长在古建筑和民俗方面颇有研究，特别是对姜氏庄园所承载的历史和文化内涵有独到的认识和见解。他撰写的讲解词是下了功夫的，经过数年的再挖掘、再充实和再修改，短短几千字，使得这处建筑和其主人活灵活现、如在眼前，广受好评，赢得了专家和业内人士的高度赞许。他不仅掌握资料丰富，且有过系统研究，轻车熟路，如数家珍，对于游客提出的一些疑问，他都能一一解答。可以说，他已经把自己完全融入了姜氏庄园之中，他是这里当之无愧的专家。

past and present of this architectural masterpiece, which is a valuable and reliable data compilation for the studies of the Jiang Family Manor and an achievement of the long time efforts of Kesheng and his colleagues, reflecting the zeal, devotion and pursuit of the cultural heritage conservers to the cultural relics and museum causes. As a colleague, I am heartily happy and deeply moved by their spirits.

This also shows that the in-depth and solid cultural heritage and museum job needs workers with persistent pursuits. The cultural cause is going forward forever.

March 9, 2016, in Yulin

人生最大的快乐是在奉献中创造，克生亦如此。十多年来，他甘于平淡，耐得住寂寞，潜心钻研，淡泊名利。他坚持守候在姜氏庄园的这一方天地中，其中的酸甜苦乐，绝非外人可知晓。

随着姜氏庄园知名度的提高，参观者逐年递增，克生和同仁们尚怀一大心愿，就是想印刷发行纸质画册，使之既具收藏价值，又能深度传播，更是对姜氏庄园的永久性记载。

这项工作早已启动，他们在默默做着自己要做的事，文字整理、图标绘制、影像拍摄、资金争取等等，这便给了我执笔补述姜氏庄园文物管理所从无到有、工作人员坚持不懈提升庄园品位过程的机会。

我仔细阅读画册清样后，觉得此画册不仅史料翔实、内容丰富，而且斟句酌词、通俗精炼、画面感强。每一幅图片都注重展现庄园内涵和意蕴的营造——自然、质朴、鲜活、豪放，从"用意"到"写意"、"场景"与"角度"所表现出的与众不同，恰到好处。作品宏大处显气势，细微处见精巧，立意高远，意景相融，让人感到有"一图胜千言"的启迪意义，达到了一定的艺术高度。

《姜氏庄园》画册即将出版，是第一次以专集形式全面记录姜氏庄园前世今生的珍贵读物，是研究和佐证姜氏庄园的一份珍贵而翔实的史料印记，也是克生及其同仁长期悉心付出的结果，体现出了文物工作者对文物事业的热爱和执着与追求。作为同行，我由衷地高兴，并被他们孜孜以求的精神所感动。

由此可见，深入、扎实的文物工作，需要执着追求和无私奉献的文物工作者。博大精深的文化事业，永远在路上。

2016 年 3 月 9 日 于榆林

乔建军 / Qiao Jianjun

西北大学文博专业毕业，现任榆林市文物保护研究所所长。曾组织参与多次考古调查和发掘工作，发表和出版有《陕西子州出土商代铜器》、《米脂官庄画像石墓》等论文和专著。

姜氏莊園

Jiang Family Manor

建于清同治十年至光绪十二年

（1871 ～ 1886 年）

Built between the 10th year of Tongzhi
and 12th year of Guangxu of Qing
(1871 - 1886)

概　述

　　姜氏庄园，位于陕西省米脂县城东 15 公里处的刘家峁村，修建于清同治十年至光绪十二年（1871～1886 年），占地面积 26000 余平方米，为全国重点文物保护单位。

　　姜氏庄园，背靠峰峦，面向溪水，依山而建，恢宏大气，其主人姜耀祖（1860～1928 年）是闻名陕北的大财主。整个宅院由城垛式寨墙、马面、井楼、炮台、下院、中院、上院、仓库、碾磨院、葡萄院、鸡鸭棚、甬道等建筑构成，设计巧妙，布局严谨，结构合理，错落有致，层层相依，环环相扣，院内套院，窑内套窑，门外套门，门内有门。宅院门庭建造豪华，院落铺设讲究，匾刻、雕镂均有寓意，或阐述一个道理，或展现一片心境，可谓"求工于一笔之内，寄情于点画之间"。无处不在、无处不精的砖、木、石三雕艺术更是巧夺天工。建筑主体及局部设置无不蕴含期盼平安吉祥、耕读传家和风水理念的传统道德风范，是中华窑洞民居建筑文化的瑰宝。

　　姜氏庄园，以其独特的建筑价值与自身魅力，吸引了众多的游客、专家、学者及新闻媒体，纷纷前来探访、采风、参观、写生和宣传报道。从 20 世纪 70 年代起，影视剧《北斗》、《刘志丹与谢子长》、《延安颂》、《张思德》、《血色浪漫》、《日出日落》、《知青》、《向日葵》、《西安事变》、《延安爱情》和《盘龙卧虎高山顶》等十余部影视剧目先后在这里选景拍摄，而姜氏庄园也已经成为展现黄土民俗风情的影视拍摄基地和黄土画派的写生基地。

　　2001 年 6 月 10 日，中央电视台《东方时空·直播时刻》栏目向全球直播报道；2006 年中央电视台《走遍中国》栏目、陕西电视台国际部《影像》栏目及资讯频道《资讯宽带网》栏目、榆林电视台《文化长廊》栏目等媒体先后作了专题报道；2010 年 10 月，中央电视台《欢乐中国行》栏目主持人张蕾，现场主持制作了外景节目。一系列连续不断的探访、关注、报道，以及各级领导的重视和地方政府的着力打造，姜氏庄园吸引了五洲四海的游人，堪称"西北民居第一宅"、"窑洞建筑的典范"、"有机结合的窑洞庄园"及"世界少有的庄园窑洞建筑艺术"。

　　姜氏庄园融独特的窑洞建筑艺术和浓郁的民俗风情为一体，展现了人类文明史上罕见的黄土人文景观，是专家、学者研究陕北黄土文化的理想之地，更是广大游客前来观光、休闲、度假的绝佳之处。

Brief Introduction

The Jiang Family Manor located at Liujiamao Village 15 km to the east of the seat of Mizhi County, Shaanxi Province was built between the tenth year of Tongzhi Era and twelfth year of Guangxu Era (1871-1886), covering an area of over 2.6 ha. It is listed as a Major Historical and Cultural Site Protected at the National Level.

Leaning against the mountains and facing the flowing brook, Jiang Family Manor is built impressive and magnificent. Its owner, whose name is Jiang Yaozu (1860-1928), was a famous rich man in the northern Shaanxi. The entire manor consists of the enclosing walls with battlements, bastions, well castle, cannon batteries, the lower, middle and upper wards, barns, mill courtyard (for processing grains), grape yard, poultry stables, corridors, etc. The designing of the architectural compound is ingenious, the layout is compact, the structure is reasonable, the arrangement of the buildings is rhythmic, the courtyards, caves and doorways are assembled skillfully. The courtyards and doorways are designed luxuriously and the grounds are paved elaborately; all of the room names, inscriptions and carvings have their connotations, some of which make certain senses, and some depict feelings; the carvings made of brick, wood and stone seen everywhere all show outstanding craftsmanship. The overall planning and the detail settings all hint the traditions of longing for peace and prosperity and farming while studying, and the idea of *fengshui*-geomancy. The Jiang Family Manor is a masterpiece of the cave-style domestic architecture of China.

By its unique architectural value and charms, the Jiang Family Manor attracts innumerous tourists, experts, scholars and journalists to come to visit, collect anecdotes and tales, make onsite drawings and gather news. Since the 1970s, many movies and TV plays have been shot with Jiang Family Manor as locations, and here has become the bases of the movie and TV play shooting and the onsite drawing of the "Loess School" of Painting reflecting the customs and folklores of the Loess Plateau.

On June 10, 2001, the LiveShow column of the "Oriental Horizon" program of CCTV globally broadcasted the Jiang Family Manor; in 2006, the

"Across China" Program of CCTV, the "Image" column of the International Department and the "Information Wideband" column of the Business Information Channel of Shaanxi TV and the "Cultural Gallery" column of Yulin TV all made subject reports for the Jiang Family Manor. In October 2010, Zhang Lei, the anchorperson of the "Happy in China" column, made the onsite show in the Jiang Family Manor. These series of visits and reports attracted tourists from all over the world, and made it "the No. 1 of the domestic architecture in northwestern China", "the paradigm of cave dwellings", "the organically assembled cave and manor" and "globally rare cave and manor architectural artwork."

The Jiang Family Manor concentrated the unique cave architectural art and thick local folk customs together, and shows the Loess Plateau humanity landscape which is special in the history of the human civilization. It is an ideal site for the experts and scholars to study the Loess Culture in northern Shaanxi and a perfect sightseeing scene for the tourists to visit and spend their holidays.

庄园全景（由东南向西北摄）
Full-view of the Jiang Family Manor (SE-NW)

历史沿革

　　姜氏庄园主人属米脂姜姓支系。始祖姜思政，字弼臣，是陕西华阴县东班庄人，木匠，约在明嘉靖年间因故流落米脂，定居县城南寺坡，娶妻班氏，繁衍生息，后世兴旺，四百余年后已传衍到第十六、十七世，后人遍及刘家峁、姜兴庄、桥沟、沙坪上、七里庙等十几个村庄及周边县区。

　　刘家峁村以姜姓为主，支系纷繁，十二世姜耀祖

是其重要一支。其家族的兴盛始于祖父姜安邦（十世）、父亲姜锦堂（十一世），主要通过务农、经商、典买土地、放高利贷、收取地租等方式聚敛了大量土地和财富，到姜耀祖时已拥有土地上万亩，粮食数千石，金银充足，具备了大兴土木的实力。

　　姜锦堂晚年得子姜耀祖，视若掌上明珠，从小培养他习文和处世之道，使其较早成熟，十多岁便帮父亲掌管家事。姜锦堂考虑到旧居隘窄，于清同治十年（1871年）选址牛家梁向阳山湾，破土兴工修建宅院。期间，姜锦堂将许多修建事项交由12岁的姜耀祖掌管料理。此时，姜锦堂因年事渐高，不胜操劳，于清光绪四年（1878年）去世，享年61岁。宅院修建工程则继续由姜耀祖主持，并于清光绪十二年（1886年）孟冬竣工落成。此后的数十年间，此庄园一直由姜耀祖及其子孙居住，家丁仆役众多，库室充盈，过着闲适富足的地主庄园生活。

　　1946年，土地改革的潮流冲击了这个地主家族，其土地、财产除适量留给本家外，大部分在"土改"中分配给了贫雇农、烈军属和财粮部门使用。新中国成立以后，庄园内有十余户人家居住共用，一直延续到20世纪中叶。由于多家居住，各户自行其是，整

全国重点文物保护单位标志
The Sign of the Major Historical and Cultural
Site Protected at the National Level

The History and Development of the Jiang Family Manor

The owner family of the Jiang Family Manor is a branch of the Jiang Clan in Mizhi County. The first ancestor, whose name is Jiang Sizheng and his courtesy name is Bichen, originally a carpenter of Dong Banzhuang Village in Huayin County, Shaanxi, traveled to Mizhi during the Jiajing Era (1522-1566) of the Ming Dynasty and settled down at Nansipo in the seat of Mizhi County, where he married a woman from the Ban Family and started a prospering lineage. Four centuries later, his descendants of the sixteenth and seventeenth generations have been spreading to the more than a dozen villages including Liujiamao, Jiangxingzhuang, Qiaogou, Shapingshang, Qilimiao Villages in Mizhi County and in nearby counties and regions.

Jiang Family is the most people in the residents of Liujiamao Village; this family has many branches, and that of Jiang Yaozu, who belonged to the twelfth generation (since Jiang Sizheng), is an important one. The flourishing of his branch was started from his grandfather, Jiang Anbang (the tenth generation) and his father, Jiang Jintang (the eleventh generation), who gathered large amount of wealth by farming, doing commercial business, farmland dealing, lending money at usury, renting farmland, and so on; down to the generation of Jiang Yaozu, the Jiang Family had owned over a dozen thousand *mu* (1 ha is 15 *mu*) of farmland, thousands of *shi* (1 *shi* is about 60 kg) of grains, and plenty of gold and silver, and enough fund to build an elegant manor.

Jiang Jintang had his son, Jiang Yaozu, at his old age, so he paid much attention to this son; he taught his son cultural classes and the social manners, which made his son mature quickly; Jiang Yaozu began to help his father to manage the family affairs when he was an early teenager. Considering the narrow old house, Jiang Jintang chose a site at a south-facing slope at Niujialiang to build his new mansion in the tenth year of Tongzhi Era (1871) of the Qing Dynasty. During this period, Jiang Jintang assigned many engineering issues to Jiang Yaozu, who was only 12 years old at that time, to manage. Before the completion of the construction of the new manor, Jiang Jintang died of overwork in the fourth year of Guangxu Era (1878) at the age of 61. The management of the construction of

体建筑只能自然存在，年久失修，自然风化，加之"文革"中横扫"四旧"的人为破坏，一些建筑局部被损，但整体建筑尚属完好。

20 世纪 80 年代，随着专家、学者们的探访和关注，以及摄影家们的光临和新闻媒体的报道，姜氏庄园引起了地方政府和有识之士的高度重视。1999 年，米脂县人民政府决定将姜氏庄园列为县级重点文物保护单位。2000 年，米脂县人民政府发出了关于"姜氏民宅"为县级文物保护单位的通知。2001 年 12 月 12 日，中共米脂县委常委会研究决定，成立米脂县姜氏庄园文物管理所，逐步由私人居住使用向文物管理部门过渡。2003 年 9 月 24 日，姜氏庄园被公布为陕西省重点文物保护单位。2004 年

4 月 12 日，米脂县人民政府成立了由县人大常委会高亚林副主任为组长，桥河岔乡镇府、文化局、文管所、村委会以及财政、公证等相关单位和人员组成的"征购姜氏庄园工作组"；同年 4 月 28 日，管理人员进驻姜氏庄园，5 月 1 日，庄园正式对外开放，并于 9 月被榆林市委、市政府确定为"爱国主义教育基地"。2005 年，西安美术学院确定姜氏庄园为"黄土画派写生基地"。2006 年 5 月 25 日，姜氏庄园被国务院公布为第六批全国重点文物保护单位。2007 年，米脂县人民政府对姜氏庄园实施了第一期维修保护工程，2009 年，新建了停车场，2015 年，对西南寨墙进行了抢救性维修，旅游环境得到进一步改善。

庄园全景（由东南向西北摄）
Full-view of the Jiang Family Manor(SE-NW)

the new manor was taken over by Jiang Yaozu and finally completed in the tenth moon of the twelfth year of Guangxu Era (1886). In the decades since then, Jiang Yaozu and his descendants were living in this manor as a rich and sedate landlord family with large numbers of armed retainers and servants and full barns and warehouses.

In 1946, the tide of "Land Reform" attacked this landlord family; except of a part of the farmlands and belongings were kept for the Jiang Family, most of them were distributed to the former poor peasants, farm laborer, families of the revolutionary martyrs and soldiers, as well as governmental departments. After the founding of the People's Republic, this manor was occupied by a dozen or so families, until the mid 1990s. Occupied by so many families, this manor did not have a unified amending and maintaining plan, therefore it could only exist as it was; because of the years of natural weathering and the artificial damaging in the "Great Cultural Revolution", some parts of the manor were spoiled but generally, the whole manor was still preserved intact.

In the 1980s, along with the visits and concerns of the experts and scholars, and the revealing of the photographers and reporting of the journalists, the Jiang Family Manor drew attentions of the local government and wise people. In 1999, the Jiang Family Manor was listed as the Historical and Cultural Site Protected at the County Level by the Mizhi County Government and proclaimed this decision in 2000. On December 12, 2001, the Standing Committee of the Mizhi County Committee of the Chinese Communist Party made a decision to establish the Commission for Preservation of the Cultural Relics of the Jiang Family Manor and gradually change this architectural complex from a private dwelling to a cultural relic monument. On September 24, 2003, the Jiang Family Manor is proclaimed as Historical and Cultural Site Protected at the Provincial Level by the Shaanxi Provincial Government. On April 12, 2004, the Mizhi County Government established the "Jiang Family Manor Purchasing Work Group" lead by Gao Yalin, the vice chairman of the Standing Committee of the People's Congress of Mizhi County, and consisting of the cadres and clerks from the government of the Qiaohecha Township, Cultural Bureau, Commission for Preservation of Ancient Monuments, Village Committee and the financial and notary departments; on April 28 of the same year, the managing personnel stationed into this manor, and on May 1, the manor was opened to the public formally and nominated as the "Patriotism Education Base" by the Yulin Municipal Committee of Chinese Communist Party and Yulin Municipal Government in September of the same year. In 2005, Xi'an Academy of Fine Arts defined the Jiang Family Manor as the base of the onsite drawing of the "Loess School" of painting. On May 25, 2006, the State Council listed the Jiang Family Manor into the sixth set of the Major Historical and Cultural Sites Protected at the National Level. In 2007, Mizhi County Government conducted the first term of maintenance and conservation project to the Jiang Family Manor. In 2009, the new parking lot was built, and in 2015, the southwest enclosure wall was repaired, the touring condition was further perfected.

创业发家

　　姜耀祖是陕北富甲一方的大财主，拥有土地上万亩，年储粮数千石，财源广进，积蓄丰厚，自有实力大兴土木。可姜家的兴盛并非起自姜耀祖，而始于其祖父姜安邦。

　　曾祖父姜怀德（九世）曾中武举，当过地方小吏。其时家境并不富裕，到祖父姜安邦（十世）时才逐步兴旺发达。姜安邦年轻时曾给杨家沟的地主马良打工，他为人忠厚，聪明能干，深得马良夫妇的赏识。马良将女儿许配予他，并将常年索要不回的旧账和地租归他所有。姜安邦秉性刚毅，才智过人，将所有的欠账和地租全部收回。此后他便小有资本，在圪针店（当时属米脂，今为绥德吉镇）开商铺"崇德号"做买卖，此时，马良不幸病故，由操持家务的马嘉乐主持为妹妹与姜安邦完婚。

　　姜安邦善于审时度势，以贩卖软米、砂锅和棺木的生意发家。清道光二年（1822年），陕北遭遇瘟疫，横尸遍野，人们用砂锅熬制中药、做"纸火盆"，安葬死人得做棺木，"过事"要吃软米糕。因此，软米、砂锅、棺木价格暴涨。姜安邦不断往返于米脂和圪针店之间做这挣钱的生意，财源广进，成了当地的首富。其娶妻四房，生有四子，前三子早年病逝，大部分家

姜耀祖墓碑正面
Front View of Jiang Yaozu's Tomb Tablet

The Starting and Flourishing of the Family

As one of the richest landlords in northern Shaanxi, Jiang Yaozu owned tens of thousands of *mu* of farmlands and earned thousands of *shi* each year; this strong financial power and huge savings naturally made Jiang Yaozu manage this magnificent engineering. However, the flourishing of the Jiang Family was not started by him but by his grandfather, Jiang Anbang.

Jiang Yaozu's great-grandfather, whose name is Jiang Huaide (the ninth generation of the Jiang Family since Jiang Sizheng moved to Mizhi), has graduated in the imperial military examination and was assigned as low-ranking local official. However, when he was the head of the household, his family was not rich; down to the generation of Jiang Anbang (the tenth generation), the grandfather of Jiang Yaozu, the Jiang Family began to prosper. When Jiang Anbang was young, he was employed by Ma Liang, a landlord at Yangjiagou Village, where Ma appreciated his loyalty, honesty and intelligence and married his daughter to Jiang Anbang, and transferred the loans and land rents to be returned and paid by the borrowers and tenants in the future to him. Since then,

Jiang Anbang accumulated the first capital, and opened a shop named "Chongde (Admiring Virtue)" at Gezhendian Town (present-day Jizhen Town, Suide County, belonged to Mizhi County at that time).

Jiang Anbang was good at judging the situation and seizing the opportunities; his business was mainly trading and selling broomcorn millet, casseroles and coffin boards. In the second year of Daoguang Era of the Qing Dynasty (1822), northern Shaanxi was attacked by a plague, by which many people were killed. To concoct herbal medicine and to sacrifice the dead, the people needed casseroles; to bury the dead, they needed coffins; to entertain the attendants of the funeral affairs, broomcorn millet cake was the main food. Therefore, the prices of these three merchandises were rapidly rising. Jiang Anpang earned huge money by this chance by trading these goods back and forth between the Mizhi County seat and Gezhandian Town and became the richest landlord in that place. He had four sons, but three of them died at very young ages, so he left most of his businesses, in which there were over 6000 *mu* (more than 400 ha) of farmlands, as legacy to Jiang Jintang, who was his fourth son.

Jiang Jintang was also intelligent, diligent and thrifty as his father. He hired farmers and laborers, but he also worked in the farmlands personally and carried bricks and soil for amending the houses, and picked up donkey dung run into on the way and brought back to his farmlands as fertilizer. His home stored plenty of grains, but he forbade anyone to throw the burnt millet crust away. There is an anecdote about him saying that one day, a beggar came to

姜耀祖
Jiang Yaozu

姜耀祖墓碑背面
Back View of Jiang Yaozu's Tomb Tablet

随后让管家盛五升谷米给讨饭的带上。这件往事说明，姜家的富裕是靠勤俭得来的。他继续靠放贷、典地、买地的方法聚敛土地，在刘家峁及周边村庄、县区内（如李家坪、张岔、七里庙、牛沟、王坪、桃镇、圪宗则沟、高鸿寺沟及绥德、佳县等邻县一些村庄）也都置有土地。每年秋冬收回租米 2000 余石，骡队整整驮运一冬，仍有部分租粮存放于吉镇和米脂县城等地。当时吉镇半数商铺都由他家经营，故有"姜家半条街，马家（杨家沟）半条街"的传说，而在桃花峁和米脂县城也有他家经营的商铺。

其时，姜锦堂正值壮年，精明强干，如日中天，将商铺、土地经营得越发兴旺。时过数年，姜锦堂大兴土木、新修宅院，而这时，他已年事渐高，便将许多修建事项和家事交由 12 岁的儿子姜耀祖掌管料理，其用意是让他尽早成熟。

姜耀祖，字硕甫，生于清咸丰十年（1860 年），捐过从五品文散官——奉直大夫。他自幼秉承耕读传家祖训，就读私塾，天资聪慧，过目成诵，尤爱好诗赋，被先生称为"可造之才"。其为人性格刚毅，每遇不平事敢于出头，却并不欺贫凌弱。姜耀祖虽继承了丰厚家业，但他仍秉承祖训，勤俭持家，恪守商家经营之道，艰辛创业，使土地增加、商铺扩大，生意更加兴隆。每隔半年他便要坐上骡轿往返于圪针店和米脂县城之间，查看商铺经营情况，财源似滚雪球般源源不断，每年收银数十万两之多，积蓄空前丰厚，声名鹊起，富甲一方，并曾盛传姜耀祖戏言："我家的元宝从刘家峁能摆放到米脂县城。"这个传说虽有夸张之意，但足以说明姜家雄厚的家业和实力。

姜氏发家兴盛，是三代人勤俭持家、艰辛创业、不懈努力的必然结果。

业自然留于四子姜锦堂，当时拥有土地 2000 余垧。

姜锦堂像父亲一样精明能干、勤苦节俭。家中虽雇工干活，可他自己仍上山劳动，为修缮窑舍亲自背石挑土，出山时路遇干驴粪蛋都要脱下布袍包起带到地头；家里虽有吃不完的存粮，可连锅巴也不让倒掉。相传有一日，姜家来了一个讨饭的，主人姜锦堂吩咐管家端来一碗锅巴给他，可讨饭的不吃，口称要吃好一点的，姜锦堂沉思片刻二话没说，端起这碗锅巴倒上开水，当着讨饭人的面大口大口地吃得不剩一点，

the Jiang Family Manor and begged for something to eat. Jiang Jintang told his steward to give the beggar a bowl of burnt millet crust. But the beggar complained that this is not a good meal, and he wanted a better one. Jiang Jintang did not say anything but added some water into the bowl and ate the burnt millet crust himself, and then let the steward scoop five liters of new millet to give to this beggar. This anecdote told us that the wealth of the Jiang Family was got from saving every trivial thing. He was gradually enlarging his farmlands by loaning money, renting farmland and other means, and owned farms at Liujiamao and the nearby villages and counties, such as Lijiaping, Zhangcha, Qilimiao, Niugou, Wangping, Taozhen, Gezongze Gully, Gaohongsi Gully and some villages in Suide and Jiaxian Counties. Each year, his farms yielded over 2000 *shi* (about 120 tons) of grains, which should be transported by his mule caravans back to his manor, and the transportation could last as long as the entire winter, or even could not finish, so some harvests had to be stored at Jizhen Town and Mizhi County seat, or other places. At that time, half of the shops in Jizhen Town were run by Jiang Jintang, so at that time there was a saying that "Half of the street is (occupied by) the Jiang Family, and (the other) half of the street is (occupied by) the Ma Family (Jiang's in-law)". At Taohuamao and the Mizhi County seat, there were also shops run by Jiang Family.

At that time, Jiang Jintang was at his best age, his intelligence and smartness ran his businesses rapidly flourishing. Some years later, he saved enough deposit to build the new manor, and therefore he started the designing and planning. However, he found that he was aging and he handed over many engineering affairs to his son, Jiang Yaozu who was just 12 years old, in order to make him mature as early as possible.

Jiang Yaozu, whose courtesy name is Shuofu, was born in the tenth year of Xianfeng Era of the Qing Dynasty (1860), and has obtained a civil official title "*Fengzhi Dafu* (Grand Master for Forthright Service)" of sub-fifth rank by contribution (donating money or grains to the government). He strictly followed the family instruction of "farming without forgetting studying", and began to study at private school when he was very young; he had very good memory and strong interests on poetry, and his tutor regarded him as a "promised talent." He has firm and decisive characters, and liked to do justice when he ran into unfair affairs. He succeeded substantial legacy, but he was still holding the thrifty principle and working hard on increasing the farmlands and businesses. Every half a year, he would go to the county seat and other places to oversee the managing situation of the businesses by mule litter. Each year, his farms and businesses earned several hundreds of thousands of taels of silver, by which he accumulated peerless wealth and got great fame. It is said that Jiang Yaozu has said that "if I line up the silver ingots one by one from my house, the line can reach the county seat." This saying may be somehow exaggeration, but it still showed the strong economic strength of the Jiang Family.

The flourishing of the Jiang Family was the result of the thrifty, hard working and relentless efforts of the three generations of the household heads of the Jiang Family.

庄园建造

　　姜氏庄园修造始于姜耀祖之父姜锦堂。姜锦堂54岁时开始兴修宅院，选址牛家梁山湾作为庄基地，于清同治十年（1871年）破土兴工。由于姜锦堂年老体衰，不胜操劳，便将许多修建事项交由12岁的姜耀祖掌管料理。清光绪四年（1878年），姜锦堂去世，享年61岁。由此，这副兴工不久、规模浩大的庄园修建工程重担就全部落在了19岁的姜耀祖肩上。姜耀祖见解独到，在父亲设想的基础上，发挥才智，遍访陕北名门豪宅和山西晋商富室，问询各地高师名匠，博采众长，并融入了自己的理念，形成了以三层套院为主体的建筑设计方案。先打井后砌墙，依山势由下而上逐层修建。"一切布置都由公独出心机"，巧妙地将陕北黄土高原传统的窑洞建筑结构与京城、晋中的四合院模式融为一体，建成

了独具风格的黄土高坡民宅，"其规模之宏敞新颖，吾陕北所仅有，所谓博大精神，与众不同也"，"建筑自动工以至竣工约十五六年"。修建宅院的过程中，姜耀祖雇请了县内外许多高师名匠，诸如石工马鸣骏、王宝贵及木工李凤飞等，普工主要是乡邻村民，通常上工数十人，付给银两及粮食做工钱。建筑所用石料均是在山下沟道石场中采挖。当时并无炸药，全靠锤凿、撬杠等简陋的工具人工开凿取石，然后再一块块背上高坡。建造期间的十余年，耗粮近万石，食盐近万斤，用工二十余万天，动土上万方，用石万千块，砖瓦木料难以数计，可见其规模之大，用工之多，耗资之巨。可以说，这座历经16年漫长时间建造的窑洞庄园，是陕北数百名工匠师们用血汗筑成的。

The Construction of the Manor

The construction of the Jiang Family Manor was started by Jiang Jintang, the father of Jiang Yaozu. He chose the hill slope at Niujialiang as the location of the new manor and broke the ground in the tenth year of Tongzhi Era (1871) of the Qing Dynasty when he was 54 years old. Because he was too old to carry out all of the affairs about the construction, he handed over many affairs to Jiang Yaozu who was only 12 years old at that time to manage and supervise. In the fourth year of Guangxu Era (1878) of the Qing Dynasty, Jiang Jintang died at the age of 64. Since then, this heavy task was transferred to the hand of Jiang Yaozu, who was just 19 years old. Jiang Yaozu had innovative ideas; based on his father's designs, he visited the houses of the famous rich families in northern Shaanxi and the residences of the rich merchants in Shanxi, and asked for advices from the famous architects and craftsmen, absorbed the favorable characters of the mansions he visited and modified with his own developments, and finally made the design of the manor with three tandem wards as the main body. The water well was dug first and then the well castle and enclosure walls were built; the entire manor was arranged along with the terrain and built against the hill slope one layer by one layer from bottom to top. "Every detail is designed by the master (Jiang Yaozu)", he smartly integrated the cave dwellings, which is the typical style of the domestic architecture in the Loess Plateau area of northern Shaanxi, and the *siheyuan* (quadrangle complex), the typical residence style in the metropolitan areas, together into his manor and constructed this architectural complex with unique style. "the magnificence and originality of this mansion are matchless in our northern Shaanxi; its spaciousness and elegance are different from that of any others." This engineering lasted for about fifteen or sixteen years. During the construction, Jiang Yaozu hired many high-level architects and handicraft masters, such as the famous masons Ma Mingjun and Wang Baogui, the famous carpenter Li Fengfei, and so on; the laborers were mainly the local villagers, whose salaries were silver and grains. The stone blocks used in the construction were all quarried from the valley below the construction site; at that time, explosives were not used, every stone block was hewn out by hammers, iron drills and wedges, and carried up to the slope by the laborers. The construction of this manor spent about a dozen thousand *shi* of grains, about 10 thousand *jin* (5 tons or so) of salt, over 200 thousand man-days, dug and refilled tens of thousands of cubic *chi* (27 cubic *chi* is 1 cu m) of earth, laid innumerous stone blocks, bricks and tiles, and used innumerous wood materials. We may say that this huge cave manor completed by a long time of 16 years was built of the blood and sweat of the hundreds of craftsmen and laborers of the northern Shaanxi.

建筑特点

姜氏庄园从山脚到山顶分为三个既连通又独立的院落，组成一个大型窑洞群体。

第一层是下院，坐西北向东南，其旧时长期由管家居住，故又称管家院、铺子院。院前用块石垒砌9.5米高的寨墙，卫护整个庄园，上筑城垣垛口。道路从山麓直上再向左折到寨门。路面宽4米，两旁为步行石阶，中间用片石排列竖插，既方便车马通行，又利于泄洪排水。寨门为拱洞，门额石匾由姜耀祖题书"大岳屏藩"四字，字体工整遒劲。入门经高大涵洞，拾级登临至下院外平台。下院大门为硬山顶，猫头滴水，水磨青砖砌筑，犀头砖雕"福禄寿喜"，彩绘斗拱额枋，门额镶嵌"大夫第"行楷木匾（姜耀祖捐过从五品文散官——奉直大夫，故有此匾）。门洞两侧有精雕抱鼓石。大门一侧连接倒座石板铺顶的马棚。院内正面为三孔石窑，正窑北侧有通往中院和上院的石砌阶梯暗道。院外东侧既是寨墙，又为井楼（外看为楼，内部为窑），内有一口从山下一直砌石而上的深井，井深33.3米，井口安手摇辘轳，井旁置大型贮水石槽和洗衣槽。

贮水石槽上方所对应的窑顶留有方口，上面可以用桶从水槽中吊水，直接挑至中院和上院。窑顶箍有习武练功用的石锁，墙壁建有藏匿财宝的石洞，小窑顶部留有拉响铜铃的报警口设置，窑上方设有吊放轿子的梁架，地下有泄洪暗道。井楼构建巧妙、功能颇多，与东寨墙"马面"连为一体，可居高临下，守望寨门、宅院。

第二层为中院，坐东北向西南。由下院大门西侧道路经石砌涵洞向上登临，路面铺石同前。中院门前西南耸立长31、高10米的石砌寨墙，围护宅院西南，有涵洞通道可上寨墙顶部，涵洞门额上有"保障"二字石匾。大门在院前正中，硬山顶，明暗柱，斗拱举架，青砖山墙，雀替、驼峰、额枋彩绘。走廊两侧有"福"、"寿"字样砖雕和门墩石狮，门额镶嵌"武魁"匾（姜耀祖二叔父姜鹰翔曾中武举）。门内院前正中砌水磨青砖影壁式圆门，外圆内方，上有顶饰，砖雕浮刻精细、典雅。中院为客厅，比之下院更加宽敞明亮。方形石板铺地，两侧各为三间大厢房，附小耳房。厢房两架梁，筒瓦硬山顶，

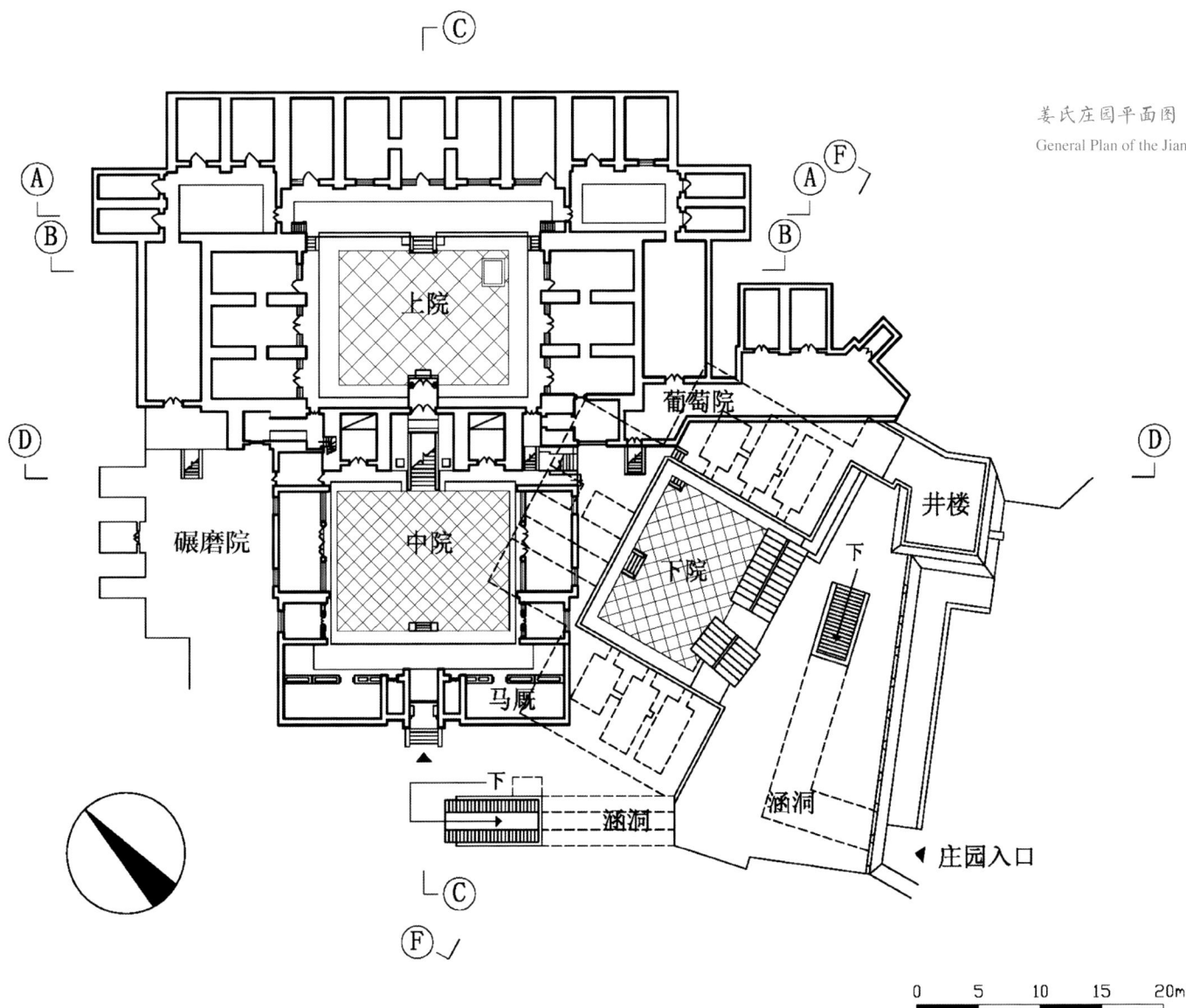

姜氏庄园平面图
General Plan of the Jiang Family Manor

上院

葡萄院

碾磨院

中院

下院

井楼

马厩

下

下

涵洞

涵洞

庄园入口

0 5 10 15 20m

本章节测绘图均引自王军《西北民居》，中国建筑工业出版社，2009 年。

上院纵剖面图（A-A）
The Longitudinal Section of the Upper Ward (A-A)

上院纵剖面图（B-B）
The Longitudinal Section of the Upper Ward (B-B)

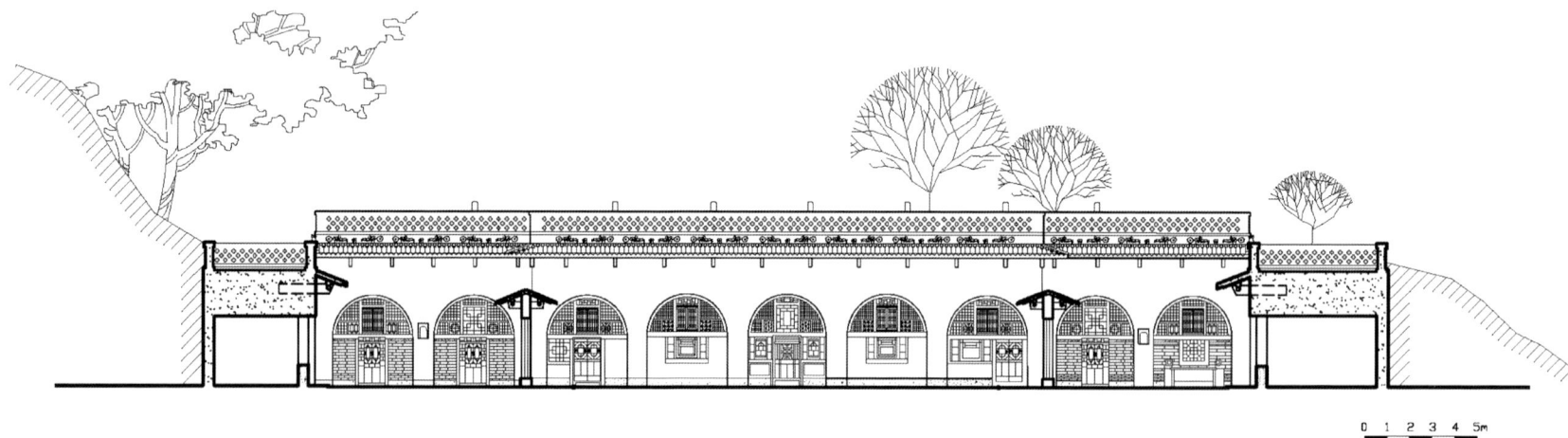

0 1 2 3 4 5m

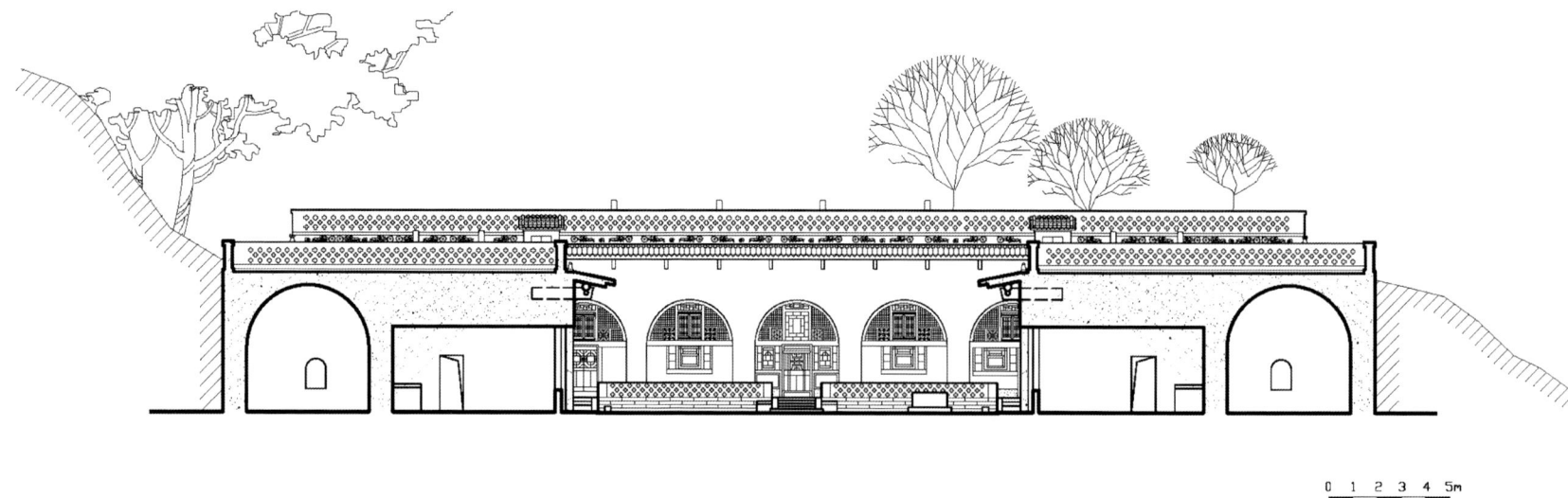

0 1 2 3 4 5m

The Characteristics of the Architectural Complex

From bottom to top of the hill slope, the Jiang Family Manor consisted of three independent but interdependent wards, which formed a large-scale cave dwelling and courtyard complex.

The first story is the Lower Ward, which is facing southeast. In the past, it is the dorm of the steward, so it was also called as "the steward yard." The outer enclosure wall in front of the Lower Ward built with stone blocks, which is 9.5 m high, is the fence of the entire manor, and has battlements on the top. The passage reaching the manor started from the hill foot and made a left turn into the gate of the manor. The passage is 4 m wide and consisting of the ramp in the middle paved with vertically lined stone pieces for the carriages and horses and the steps built with stone blocks for pedestrians flanking the ramp. This design is not only convenient for the wheeled vehicles and walking people, but also good for the discharging of rainwater. The gateway of the manor has a vaulted roof, over which is a stone board with inscription "Da Yue Pingfan (the safeguard of the Great Mountain)" written by Jiang Yaozu in sinewy style.

Entering the gate, through the long tunnel and steps, the terrace outside the entrance of the Lower Ward is arrived. The entrance of the Lower Ward is in the shape of a house with gable roof built with gray bricks and the surfaces of the walls were closely polished, the tile-ends of the eaves were decorated with cat face design. The front of the gables are decorated with brick carving of the figures of a high official, a deer, a magpie and a pine tree (symbolizing high official position, good salary, happiness and longevity) and five bats (symbolizing good fortune) surrounding a character shou (longevity), the bracket sets and lintels are painted with color designs, and above the doorway is the wooden board with the inscription "Dafu Di (Residence of the Grand Master)" in regular script. On the two sides of the doorway are two finely engraved drum-shaped doorframe-bearing stones. On the inner side of the wall beside the entrance are the horse stables with stone plank roof. In the Lower Ward, directly facing the entrance are three stone-lined cave dwellings, to the north of which is the stepped stone tunnel passage leading to the Middle and Upper Wards. Outside the Lower Ward, on the east is the well castle (seen from the outside, it is a tower but the internal are caves), in which is a deep well dug to the foot of the hill and lined with stone up to the opening; the well is 33.3 m deep, over which a hand-driven winch is set to draw water up, and large stone tanks and washing troughs

0 1 2 3 5 10m

0 1 2 3 5 10m

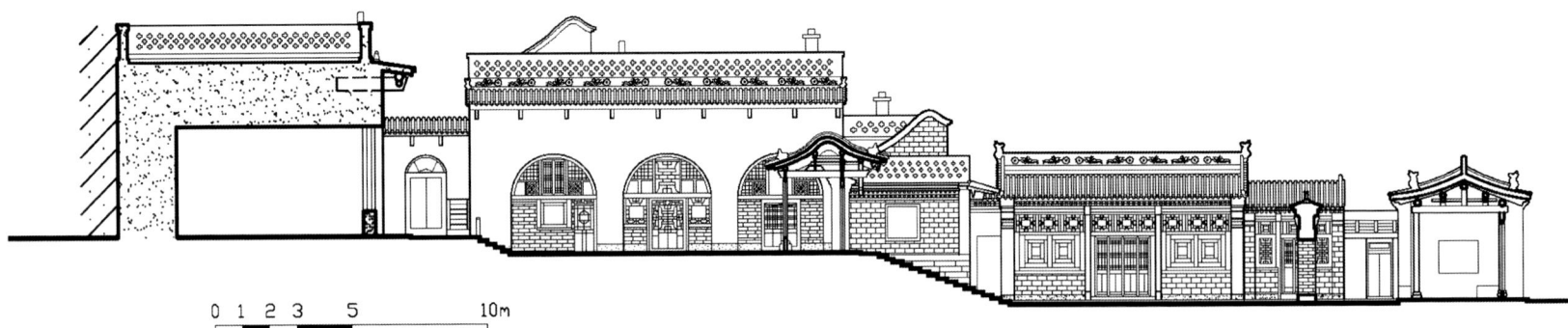

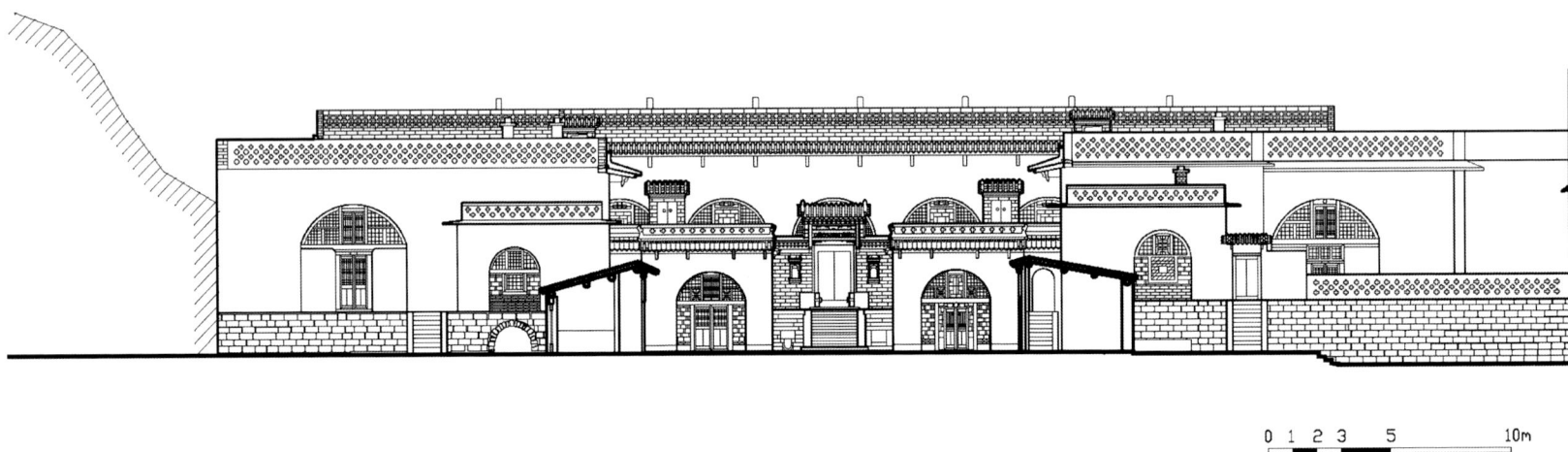

上院、中院横剖面图（C-C）
The Transverse Section of the Upper and Middle Wards (C-C)

中院纵剖面图（D-D）
The Longitudinal Section of the Middle Ward (D-D)

are set beside the well. On the roof of the well castle directly above the stone water tanks, there is an opening through which the water buckets could be roped down to take water up to the Middle and Upper Wards. On the ceiling of the well castle, stone locks for doing exercise are inserted, and on the wall, small caves for storing treasures are dug; on the top of the castle, small opening for hanging alarm bells is set, and on the ceiling, beams for hanging sedans are inserted; on the floor, floor drain is opened. The well castle is skillfully designed with multiple functions, together with the "bastions" built against the east manor wall, it safeguarded the gate and the wards.

The second story is the Middle Ward, which is facing southwest. By the passage from on the west side of the entrance of the Lower Ward through the stone vaulted tunnel going upward, the terrace of the Middle Ward is reached. The paving of the passage is in the same form as that of the passage from the hill foot to the manor gate. The outer enclosure wall 31 m long and 10 m high in front of the entrance of the Middle Ward safeguards the southwest of the manor, the top of which can be reached through a tunnel, and over the entrance of the tunnel is a stone board with the inscription "*Baozhang* (Safeguarding)". The entrance is in the middle of the front wall of the ward, which is in the form of a house with gable roof built with gray bricks, the roof of which has bracket sets to support; the sparrow brackets, post blocks and lintels are all painted with color patterns. Over the doorway, a wooden board with the inscription "*Wu Kui* (Principal Graduate of the Imperial Military Examination)" is inlayed (Jiang Yingxiang, the uncle of Jiang Yaozu, has been graduated in the Imperial Military Examination). At the center of the courtyard in the entrance is a screen gate in the shape of a short wall with a roof-shaped top and fine brick carving decorations. The Middle Ward is the place for receiving guests, so the houses in this ward are all more spacious and brighter than that in the Lower Ward. The courtyard is paved with square stone planks and flanked by a side room with three bays and an attached wing room on each side. The side rooms are two bays deep and the wing rooms are one bay deep; the roofs of the side rooms are flush gable roofs and that of the wing rooms are arch-shaped roofs. It is almost unnoticeable that the east side room is 0.2 m higher than the west side room; this arrangement is the remnant of the ancient *zhaomu* system that regarding the left side as the superior side and the east side is the upper side, reflecting the local custom. To the north of the east side room is a narrow passage reaching the

格扇木窗，窗棂美观大方；耳房一架梁，卷棚顶，铺筒瓦。令常人难以察觉的是，东厢房比西厢房高出 0.2 米，这是按照古代"昭穆之制"左为尊位而东为上位的习俗而做，隐含一种民俗在其中。东厢房北侧有小过道连接葡萄院和东仓窑，并有石砌阶梯暗道连通上院和下院。西厢房北侧小过道连通碾磨院、西仓窑和应急外遁的窨子地道。中院正中上方是通向上院的门楼，两侧各一孔窑洞（称"围窑"）。中院外东侧寨墙下有鸡鸭棚。

第三层即是上院，是整个建筑群的主宅，由主人居住，坐东北向西南。上院门楼在院前正中，砖木结构垂花门，柱梁门框举架，雕花彩绘，卷棚瓦顶。

下院纵剖面图（F-F）
The Longitudinal Section of the
Lower Ward (F-F)

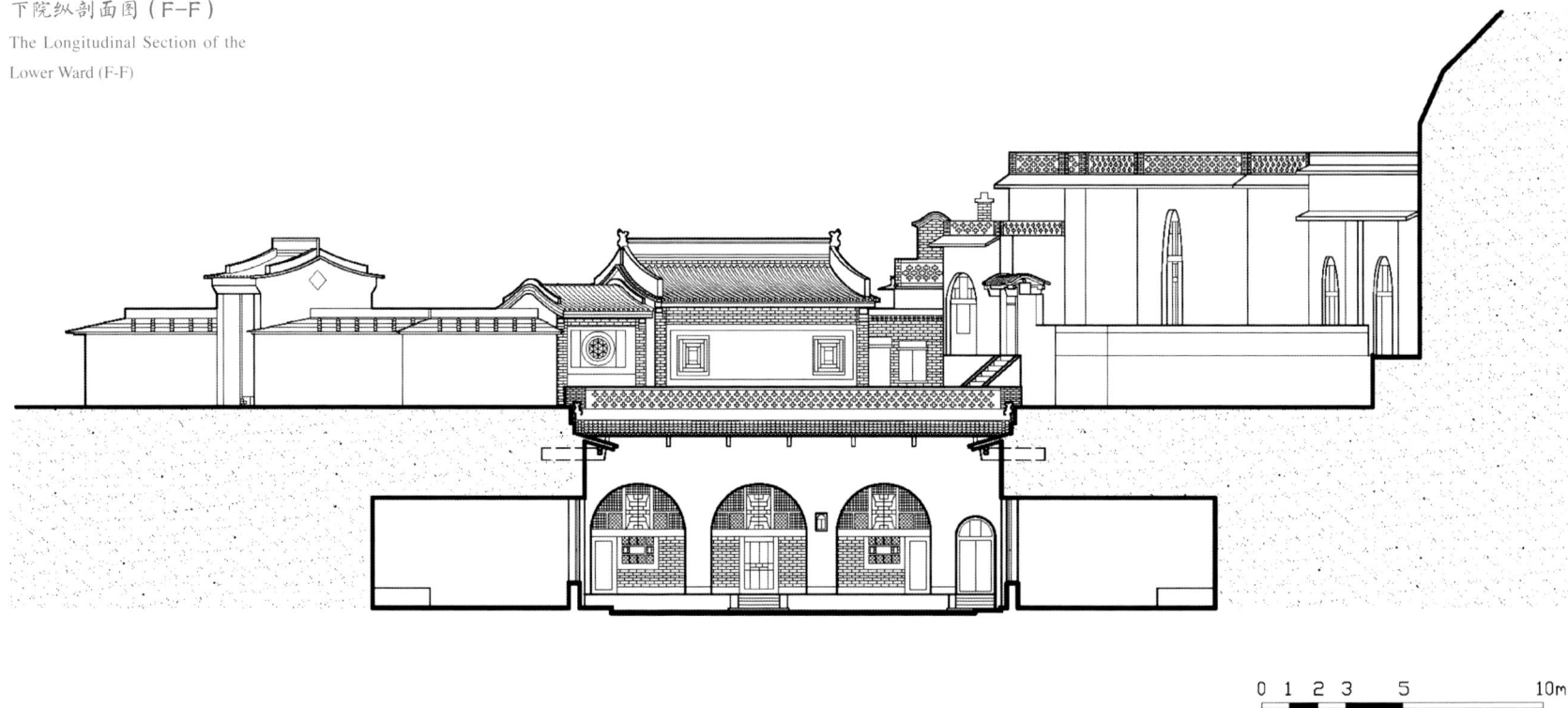

0 1 2 3　5　　　　10m

grape yard and the Eastern Barn Cave, and stone-built secret tunnels going to the Lower and Upper Wards. Another narrow passage to the north of the west side room reaches the mill courtyard, the Western Barn Cave and the escaping tunnel in case of urgent situations. In the middle of the upper part of the Middle Ward is the gate tower going to the Upper Ward, which is flanked by two caves (so-called "surrounding caves"). By the east manor wall outside the Middle Ward, poultry stables are built.

The third story is the Upper Ward, which is the main body of the entire manor facing southwest. This is the residence of the master of the Jiang Family. The entrance of the Upper Ward is in the middle of the front wall of the court, which is a festooned gate with arched roof ridge built of brick and timber, the beams, pillars, doorframe and roof truss are all painted with color decorations. The green lacquered door leaves have bronze *pushou*-doorknockers, capped nails and cloud-shaped margin fittings. It has another screen door on the inside, which has two hinged door leaves. On the walls beside the entrance, Soil Deity shrines are set. On the side walls of the doorway, the brick carvings of "Deer Running in the Pine Forest" and "Crane Crowing in the Bamboo Grove" are inlayed. In the façade of the Upper Ward, five stone-lined caves are opened abreast, each of which is 3.1 m wide, 4.5 m high and 8 m deep. The three caved in the middle are linking to each other, all of which have *kang* (heatable brick bed), wall closets, terrazzo heaths, square stone plank-paved floors,

double-leaf doors and light windows. The five façade caves have a through porch eave supported with stone cantilevers, and on the top of the caves, a parapet with cross-shaped openings is built. Flanking the five main caves, two small courtyards are built, over the doors of which, boards with inscriptions "*Yang Lian* (Cultivating Honesty and Cleanness)" and "*Jiang Rang* (Advocating Courtesy)" are inlayed respectively. On the sides of each courtyard, elongated from the front wall of the five main caves, two caves are opened, which formed the so-called "four hidden caves"; plus the five main caves and the three side caves flanking them, the entire cave complex formed the typical pattern of "Five Main, Four Hidden and Six Side (Caves)" in the domestic architecture of the northern Shaanxi. Behind the side caves are two other long caves, each of which is 14 m long, leading to the two small courtyards beside the five main caves; they were called as "big pillow caves" and used as barn caves, each has 12 large stone barns (every large stone barn could store 50 *shi* of grains) and small stone barns (every small stone barn could store 1 *shi* of grains), and the two barn caves could store over 1200 *shi* of grains. On the east and west ends of the inner enclosure wall of the Upper Ward, there are small doorways: the east one leads to the Middle and Lower Wards and the west one leads to the restroom. The entire manor is built against the hillside, atop which cannon batteries were built to guard it.

The Jiang Family Manor integrated the practicalities and artistries together: it has exquisite designs and compact layout, the location against the hill is good

绿漆门扇镶铜制铺首、泡钉、云钩，连有转扇二门，门庭两侧墙上设土地神龛，廊心墙砖雕"鹿奔松林"、"鹤唳寿石"。上院正面石台阶上一线五孔石窑，宽3.1、高4.5、进深8米。正中三孔连通，均盘火炕，暖阁壁橱，水磨石灶，方形石板铺地，双门亮窗。窑面挑石穿廊，顶砌"十"字砖饰花墙，十分壮观。正窑东西两旁各设小院，门额上方分别有"养廉"、"讲让"二字。小院内正面窑洞各两孔，俗称"暗四间"，加之上院正面五孔窑、两侧各三孔厢窑，组成了陕北典型的"明五暗四六厢窑"式窑洞院落。厢窑背后是与东西小院相通的两孔窑，长14米，俗称"大枕头窑"，作储粮仓库，其内各砌大石仓12个（每仓储粮50石），上坐小石仓（每仓储粮1石），东西仓窑共可储粮1200余石。上院内围墙东西两端有小门洞，东连中院和下院，西为厕所。整个庄园背倚高山寨墙，上筑有炮台守护整个宅院。

姜氏庄园磅礴大气，集实用性与艺术性于一体，设计巧妙，布局严谨，依山而建，错落有致，对外严于防卫，院内通连方便。窑室冬暖夏凉，起居舒适得宜。它是石雕、木刻、砖塑等建筑艺术的集中展示，是黄土高原窑洞建筑的光辉范例。可以说，陕北民间工匠技艺在这里得到了高度发挥。

庄园以石建筑为主，无论是寨墙、涵洞、拱窑的垒砌，道路、台阶、院落的铺设，石锅台、石炕沿、石床、石仓的安置，还是门墩石狮、门额石刻、穿廊挑石的精雕，石水槽、石鱼水道、石马槽、拴马石的细刻，都达到了出神入化的境界，无不体现石料的合理应用和工艺处理。其水磨砖雕人物形象、鹤鹿松竹、流云花草的造型图饰，皆栩栩如生、活灵活现。门庭木刻彩绘花形、窗棂窗扇、枋额匾牌，也都与主体搭配得宜。面对如此建筑，无论对其规模格局，还是细部构筑，都让远道而来的专家、学者叹服，惊呼："高原深处有如此建筑精品，出乎想象！"因此，姜氏庄园成为陕北旅游开发的重要景点、民俗文化研究的宝贵场所。

for guarding against the outer attacks and the units in the entire manor are communicable easily. The cave dwellings are warm in the winter and cool in summer and very suitable for living. The Jiang Family Manor is a gallery exhibiting the stone sculpture, wood carving and brick carving arts and domestic architectural skills, and a splendid model of the cave courtyard dwelling of the Loess Plateau. We can say that the talents of the folk artisans and craftsmen in northern Shaanxi were fully displayed in this architecture.

The main body of the Jiang Family Manor is the masonry; either the building of the enclosure wall, tunnels, caves, the paving and building of the passages, steps and floors, the setting of the stone hearths, stone *kang* linings, stone beds and stone barns, or the carving of the doorframe bearing stones, stone boards, stone cantilevers, stone water tanks, stone fish, stone mangers and the hitching holes, all showed the superb skills and the rational application and processing of the stone materials. The motifs of the brick carvings, such as the human figures, cranes, deer, pine trees, bamboo, flying clouds, plants and flowers, are all depicted vividly. The wood carvings and color-paintings of the block and bracket sets, window grills and inscription boards are also suitably matching the architectures to which they are attached or set. To this architectural masterpiece, no matter its scale and planning or its details and structures, the scholars and experts from afar all cannot help admiring: "it could not be imagined that such an architectural artwork can appear in this remote plateau area!" Therefore, the Jiang Family Manor becomes the important sightseeing spot in the tourism industry of the northern Shaanxi and a rare location for the researches on the folklore culture.

西北民居第一宅

姜氏庄园

（解说词） 撰文：艾克生

The Jiang Family Manor

The No. 1 of the Domestic Architecture in
Northwestern China

Author: Ai Kesheng

各位来宾、各位游客：

大家好！热烈欢迎各位来姜氏庄园观光旅游！

姜氏庄园，位于陕北米脂县城东 15 公里处的刘家峁村。它修建于清同治至光绪年间（1871～1886 年），面积 26000 余平方米，为全国重点文物保护单位。

这里四面环山，峰峦叠嶂，树木葱葱，溪水潺潺，迷人的高原风光，浓郁的黄土风情，将会给您带来一个美好而愉快的心情。

Dear Ladies and Gentlemen:

How are You? Welcome to the Jiang Family Manor!

Jiang Family Manor located at Liujiamao Village 15 kilometers to the east of the seat of Mizhi County, Shaanxi Province was built between the tenth year of Tongzhi Era and twelfth year of Guangxu Era (1871-1886), covering an area of over 2.6 hectares. It is listed as a Major Historical and Cultural Site Protected at the National Level.

Surrounded the mountains and facing the flowing brook, the charming plateau scenery and thick loess style will bring you a happy feeling.

庄园全景（由西向东摄）

Full-view of the Jiang Family Manor (W-E)

　　姜氏庄园主要由三部分构成，即下院、中院和上院，与主体建筑相配套的，还有碾磨院、葡萄院、鸡鸭棚、库房、井楼、炮台、寨墙等部分。整个庄园，大到整体设计，小至局部结构，无论严密的防御体系，还是完善的水利系统，都设计得十分巧妙，形成了一个完整的配套体系。

The entire manor consists of three main parts, which are the Lower, Middle and Upper Wards, and associated with mill courtyard (for processing grains), grape yard, poultry stables, warehouses, well castle, cannon batteries, etc. The overall planning and the detail settings all show the ingeniousness of the designers, no matter the overall planning or the structural details, and the tight defense system and perfect water supplying and draining systems, all of which formed a complete dwelling complex.

上院、中院（由西南向东北摄）
The Upper and Middle Wards (SW-NE)

大家首先看到的,是屹立在我们面前雄伟壮观、巍峨挺拔的庄园寨墙。

这条寓意"龙尾"的石级通道,长45.5米,两边用0.9米宽的石板铺成步行石级,中间以小石片竖插形成石道,既能方便车马通行,亦有利于排泄雨洪,其距离相等的石棱可以起到缓冲作用。

用大石块砌成的这堵城垛式寨墙,宽24.3米,高9.5米。这里有个"不弯腰"的传说——当年修葺这堵寨墙的时候,一天,正在干活的老石匠见姜耀祖从坡下走上来,心生一计,有意将手中的钢錾落于墙下,请主家姜耀祖把钢錾捡一下,姜耀祖嘿嘿一笑,向老石匠说,"修这部地方(宅院)我连腰都不用弯,你老慢慢歇着,歇好了自己来捡",说罢扬长而上。老石匠感叹地说:"这可真是不弯腰的姜财主。"我们从这则故事可以看出姜耀祖的财大气粗。据说,修建宅院耗费小米九千余石、食盐近万斤。

寨墙(由西南向东北摄)
The Enclosure Wall (SW-NE)

石级通道(由东北向西南摄)
Stone Ramped and Stepped Passage (NE-SW)

Now, what we are seeing is the Manor wall.

This stone passage with the connotation of "Dragon Tail" is 45.5 meters in length; it is paved with stone blocks 0.9 meter wide into steps on the two sides for pedestrians, and in the middle is the ramp paved with vertically lined stone pieces for the carriages and horses and also for the draining of rainwater. The evenly arranged serrations have a function of buffering.

The manor wall with battlements built with large stone blocks is 24.3 meters wide and 9.5 meters high. About this there is an anecdote of "not to bow": when this wall was built, a working old mason saw Jiang Yaozu walk up from the hill foot, he intentionally dropped his steel chisel down to the wall bottom and wanted Jiang Yaozu to pick it up for him. But Jiang Yaozu smiled and said to this old mason: "I won't need to have a bow to build this manor! Just have your break, and then pick up your chisel by yourself." And then went up. The old mason sighed and admired: "really a Jiang landlord not bowing!" From this anecdote, we can see the fact that Jiang Family was very proud about its wealth. It is said that the construction of this manor spent over nine thousand *shi* of millet (one *shi* is about sixty kilograms), and about 10 thousand *jin* (5 tons or so) of salt.

　　这里是庄园的第一道寨门，门为拱形石洞，门额上方镶嵌有主人姜耀祖手书的"大岳屏藩"石匾，字体遒劲浑厚。从字面来看，是说庄园气势磅礴，有如同大山一般的屏障抵御外来入侵。另外，它巧妙地隐含了两代主人的名字，这里的"岳"为姜海岳，即姜耀祖，而"藩"为姜耀祖的长子姜树藩，又名姜辅文。"大"在这里作形容词，喻示主人有大山一般的实力和气度，"福泽子孙，荫庇后世"。

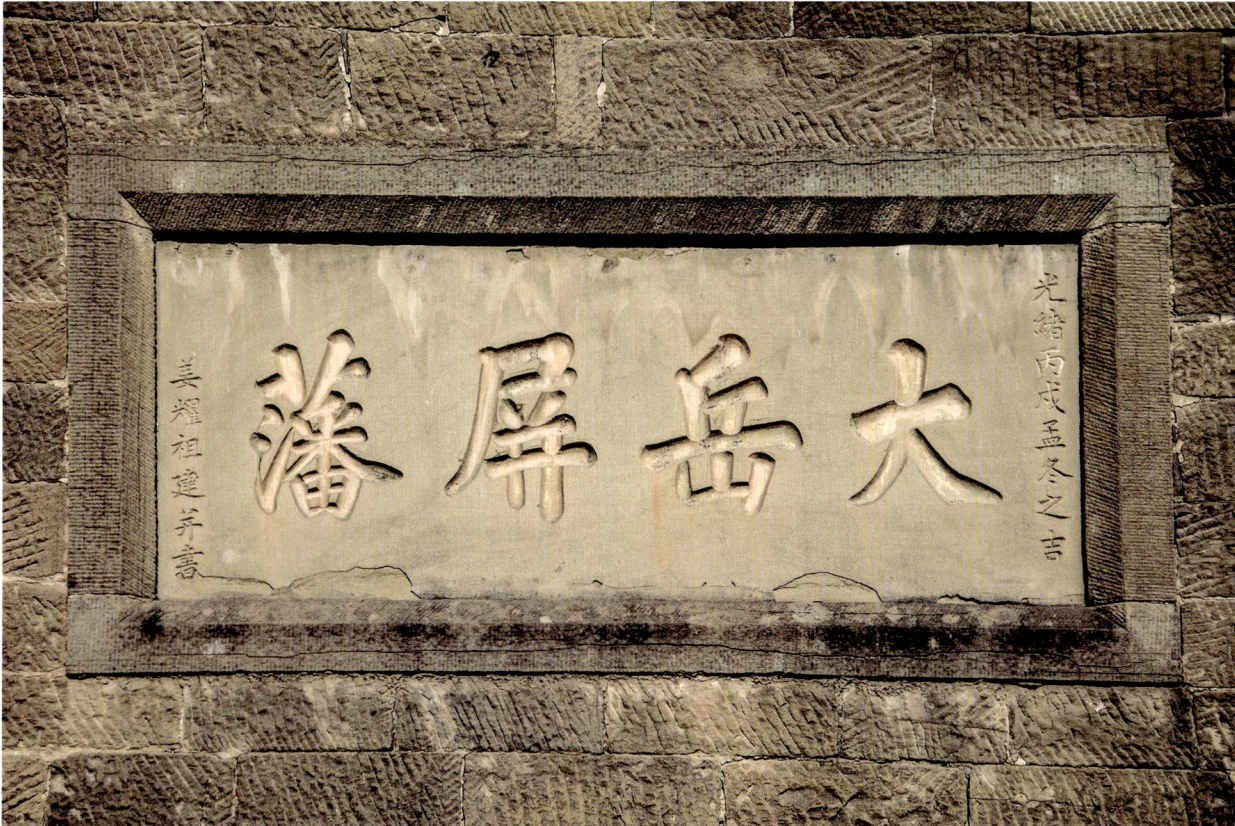

石级通道（由东向西摄）
Stone Ramped and Stepped Passage (E-W)

"大岳屏藩"石匾
The Stone Board with Inscription "*Da Yue Pingfan*
(the Safeguard of the Great Mountain)"

This is the first gate of the manor, which has a tunnel-shaped gateway with a barrel vault-shaped ceiling. Over the gateway, the stone board with inscription "*Da Yue Pingfan* (the safeguard of the Great Mountain)" written by Jiang Yaozu in sinewy style is inlayed. Literally, these four characters mean that the manor is magnificent and could guard against the outside attacks like a mountain. In addition, they implicated the names of two generations of the owners of this manor: the "*Yue*" hints Jiang Haiyue (Jiang Yaozu) and the "*Fan*" hints Jiang Shufan (also known as Jiang Fuwen), the eldest son of Jiang Yaozu. The "*Da* (big, great)" is an adjective here, implying that the owner of this manor has strength and bearing like mountains, "whose good fortune favors his descendants for endless generations."

请大家随我进入门洞——洞内折转，拱洞相连，曲径通幽，仿佛进入一个时光隧道。我们由此而上便可看到庄园的第一部分——下院和井楼。

这里的东侧建有一孔与寨墙连为一体的井窑，宽4米，高5米，其内有井深百尺（约33.3米）。井口设有手摇辘轳用来取水，水源引自山下泉眼，水质甘甜爽口。如果您有兴趣，不妨体验一下这深井取水的感受。这口结构于寨墙之内的深井，它有三个特殊意义：不出宅院就能方便取水，既可保证井水卫生，又能防止他人井内投毒，即使困守数月也无饮水之忧。

通往下院平台的涵洞（由西向东摄）
The Tunnel Going to the Terrance of the Lower Ward (W-E)

井楼（由西南向东北摄）
The Well Castle (SW-NE)

Now we are entering the gateway—this zigzag passage makes us like getting into a time tunnel. Upward from here, we are going to see the first part of the manor —the Lower Ward and the well castle.

In the east, a well castle is built engaged to the manor wall. It is 4 meters wide and 5 meters high, in which a well is dug, and it is one hundred *chi*, or about 33.3 meters deep. A hand-driven winch is set atop this well to draw water ducted from the spring downhill, and the water is sweet. If you are interested, you can try to draw water with this winch. This well enclosed in the manor made the residents conveniently use water without going out of the manor for several months, the water keep clean and outsiders poison the well. This stone water tank beside the well is two meters long and one meter high, and its type is the rare "compound tank", which is completely touched with fine chisels. It is said that when it was carried up from downhill by 32

井窑内全景
The Internal View of the Well Castle

井旁的这个宽2、高1米的巨形贮水石槽实为罕见，俗称"子母槽"，做工精细，通体以板方錾、皮条錾和一寸三錾的斜錾、一寸四錾的立水錾打制而成。据说，当年主人喊着号子，32个工匠从山脚下将大石槽抬上高坡时，突然电闪雷鸣，狂风大作，举步难行。

姜耀祖见状，急忙跪地焚香烧纸，祷告神灵，忽然大石槽向东拜了三拜，工匠们便乘风而上，将大石槽抬入井窑之内方得安放。请大家再看，留在顶部的这一方口——它是上院佣人从石槽内取水的一个道口，上面同样装有手摇辘轳，具有二级提水的功能。再看这

井窑内水井及贮水石槽
The Water Well and Stone Water Tanks in the
Well Castle

井窑内贮水石槽、铜钱形下水口
及方形检修口
The Stone Water Tanks, Bronze Coin-shaped
Floor Drain and Square Inspection Manhole
in the Well Castle

laborers, flashes and thunderbolts suddenly came as well as storm, and the laborers could not move even one step. Seeing this, Jiang Yaozu got down on his knees and burnt incenses and spirit money and prayed for the blessing of the deities. Then, the large stone water tank itself saluted to the east for three times and the laborers got together to carry it into the well castle. This square opening on the ceiling is a water transfer hole for the users in the Upper Ward to draw water from the stone water tank, and on its top, there is also a hand-driven winch. Here is the skillfully designed light window, which is built with roof tiles into the pattern of the coins of ancient China, showing the substantial property and vast wealth resource of the Jiang Family. The hole on the wall of the well castle could be used as lookout hole and embrasure: the very ignorable design reflected the strong defending sense of the manor owners. These two beams crossing over the well, what are their functions?

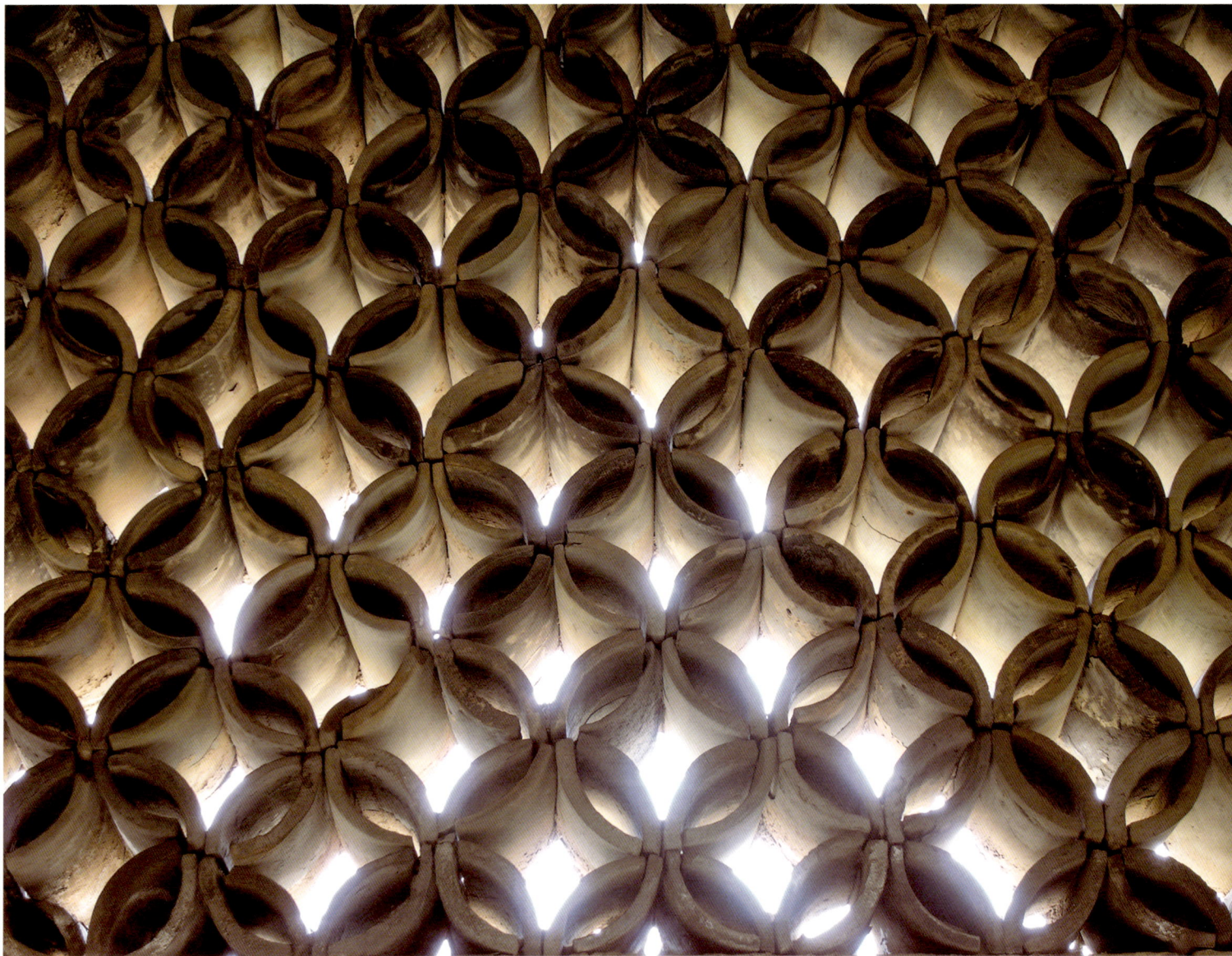

架通风透亮、构思别致、以铜钱图案组成的瓦窗，它显示主人雄厚的家业并象征滚滚财源。井窑墙壁上留有瞭望孔，既是观察哨位，又具射击功能，这隐蔽的小小设计，反映了主人极强的防范意识。井窑上方横置的两根木椽，用途是什么呢？它是主人乘坐的轿子闲置时，为了防止地面潮湿而设计在空中的吊放梁架。大家抬头看一看，箍在顶部有两个石锁。姜家乃武举世家，姜耀祖为了让他的儿子习武练功，

They were used to hang the sedans of the owners when they were not in use to separate the moisture of the floor. Now we look up to the ceiling of the well castle. On the ceiling, two stone locks are inserted. The Jiang Family has a tradition of training martial arts, and has family member graduated in the imperial military examination. To train his sons of the martial arts, Jiang Yaozu employed teachers; these two locks were used to hang sandbags for training. The side across from the well are two stone caves on the wall, which were opened for hiding treasures. The small cave beside the well is the guardhouse, on the ceiling of which there is also a small

井窑内瓦窗（局部）
The Tile Window in the Well Castle (Detail)

井窑内观察哨位及瞭望孔
The Watching Posts and Lookout Hole in the Well Castle

特意请来武教师，这两个石锁便是为了吊置沙袋练功用的。与井相对的一侧有两个石洞，这是当年藏匿财宝的地方。而井旁边的一孔小圆窑是门房，相当于现在的保卫室，其顶部同样留有一个小方口，一条绳索从方口穿过直至井窑顶部，如遇匪徒、盗贼袭击，门卫人员便立即拉响顶部铜铃报警，全院人员随即进入戒备状态或藏入暗道（即窨子）。地下设有泄洪暗道，上面留有可供方便随时清理渠道畅通的检修口。由此可见，井窑的整体设计具有双重或多重功能，可谓设计巧妙，功能颇多。

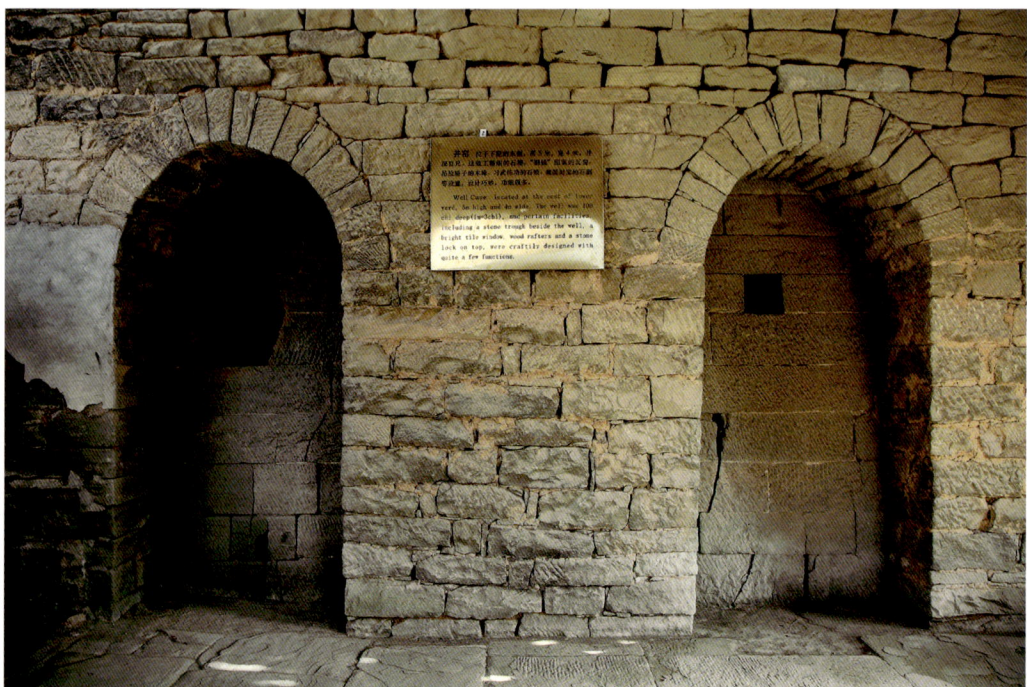

井窑内顶部的梁架及石锁
The Ceiling Beams and the Stone Locks in the Well Castle

井窑内藏匿财宝的石洞
The Stone Caves for Hiding Treasures in the Well Castle

井窑内保卫室
The Guardhouse in the Well Castle

square opening, and a rope is hanging down from the opening into the guardhouse. If the manor was attacked by gangsters or bandits, the guards in this cave could pull this rope to ring the bell on the roof to alert the people in the entire manor, and the people could either arm up or escape through the secret tunnel. Draining channels are set under the floor, and the square inspection manhole is set on the ground. Now we see that this well castle has double even multiple functions cleverly designed.

请大家随我到下院的平台——院墙上的石锁，是收缴租子时用以拴系骡马的，可以想象当年那种人欢马叫的喧闹场面。寨墙上九个垛口，九九归一，寓意宅院修造圆满顺利而告竣。形若马面的井窑寨墙，地势险峻，居高临下，扼守寨咽，可谓"一夫当关，万夫莫开"。早在20世纪70年代末，引起轰动的电影故事片《北斗》，红军攻打地主庄园的全部镜头都是在这里拍摄完成的。

Now please follow me to the terrace of the Lower Ward — the holes on the ward wall are the hitching holes used for tying mules and horses of the tenants when the Jiang Family was receiving the land rents, from which we can imagine the exciting scene at that time. The nine battlements atop the manor wall hinted the successful completion of the construction of the manor. The well castles and the bastions of the manor wall guarded the manor, the terrain of which is favorable for the defense. As early as in the late 1970s, the entire plot of the Red Army attacking the landlord's manor in the sensational feature movie *Beidou* (the Big Dipper) was shot here.

下院平台（由西向东摄）
The Terrace of the Lower Ward (W-E)

下院外墙拴系骡马的石锁（由东南向西北摄）
The Hitching Holes for Horses on the Outer Wall of the Lower Ward (SE-NW)

下院大门（由南向北摄）
The Entrance of the Lower Ward (S-N)

这是下院，叫管家院，也称铺子院，坐西北向东南。大门以水磨青砖的砖木结构砌筑，猫头滴水，五脊六兽硬山顶，墀头砖雕"福禄寿喜"、"狮子滚绣球"、"五福捧寿"、"寿桃"等图案，雕刻精细，栩栩如生，包含了主人期盼永久富贵、延年益寿、万事如意的美好愿望。"凤凰戏牡丹"木雕雀替，额枋、"一斗二升麻叶头"彩绘斗拱，搭配得宜，寓意柴米油盐。门额镶嵌"大夫第"行楷木匾，庄重大气（因姜耀祖捐过"从五品"文散官——奉直大夫而称"大夫第"）。"大夫第"三字，由清代五大书法家之一的史年佑所题，可见当年的主人既有一定社会地位，同时也注重名人效应。门额"寿桃"门簪，既牢固连接门杠，又起装饰作用，寓意"福如东海长流水，寿比南山不老松"。

下院门额"大夫第"木匾
The Lintel Board of the Entrance of the Lower Ward with Inscription "*Dafu Di* (Residence of the Grand Master)"

下院大门侧面（由东向西摄）
Side View of the Entrance of the Lower Ward (E-W)

This is the Lower Ward, which is facing southeast. It was the dorm of the steward, so it was also called as "the steward yard." The entrance of the Lower Ward is in the shape of a house with gable roof built with gray bricks and the surfaces of the walls were closely polished, the tile-ends of the eaves were decorated with cat face design. The front of the gables are decorated with brick carving of the figures of "a high official, a deer, a magpie and a pine tree (symbolizing high official position, good salary, happiness and longevity)", "a lion playing a colored silk ball", "five bats (symbolizing good fortune) surrounding a character *shou* (longevity)" and "longevity peach", which are depicted closely and vividly, reflecting the good desires of the owners for long-lasted rich and high-ranking, longevity and good fortune; the sparrow brackets with wood carving of "a phoenix playing peony flowers", the bracket sets of "one cap block holding two small blocks" and lintels are all painted with color designs, and above the doorway is the wooden board with the inscription "*Dafu Di* (Residence of the Grand Master)" in regular script, because Jiang Yaozu has obtained a civil official title "*Fengzhi Dafu* (Grand Master for Forthright Service)" of sub-fifth rank by contribution (donating money or grains to the government). The three characters "*Dafu Di*" were written by Shi Nianyou, who was one of the five most famous calligraphers of the Qing Dynasty, which reflected that the owner of this manor at that time had not only a rather high social position but also paid close attention to the "celebrity effect".

下院大门内额（由北向南摄）
The Inner Lintel of the Entrance of the Lower Ward (N-S)

下院大门墀头砖雕·狮子滚绣球
The Brick Carving of the Front of the Gable of the Entrance
of the Lower Ward: A Lion Playing a Colored Silk Ball

下院大门堰头砖雕·福禄寿喜
The Brick Carving of the Front of the Gable of the
Entrance of the Lower Ward: High Official, Deer, Magpies
and Pine Tree (Metaphors of High Official Position,
Happiness and Longevity)

下院大门墀头砖雕·五福捧寿
The Brick Carving of the Front of the Gable of the Entrance
of the Lower Ward: Five Bats (Symbol of Good Fortune)
Surrounding a Character *Shou* (Longevity)

下院大门墀头砖雕·牡丹富贵
The Brick Carving of the Front of the Gable of the Entrance
of the Lower Ward: Peony Flower

下院大门雀替木雕·凤凰戏牡丹
The Wood Carving of the Sparrow Bracket of the Entrance of
the Lower Ward: A Phoenix Playing Peony Flowers

下院大门雀替木雕·夔龙
The Wood Carvings of the Sparrow Brackets of the
Entrance of the Lower Ward: *Kui*-unipedal Dragon

门洞两侧的抱鼓石与"寿桃"门簪相互对应，又称"门当户对"。抱鼓石鼓面雕有"双龙戏珠"，边缘为一周"富贵不断头"（圆点纹）纹饰，裙袱"夔龙"，须弥座浮雕"金猴立顶"，寓意避邪镇宅。

侧壁砖廊均以书形的图案组成，意为"书香门第"。此外，下院也是办私塾的地方，又称书房院。向内门额置"夔龙"雀替，额枋、斗拱彩绘，墀头砖雕"牡丹富贵"、"福寿双全"等图案，皆栩栩如生。

下院大门抱鼓石
The Drum-shaped Doorframe Bearing Stone of the
Entrance of the Lower Ward

下院大门抱鼓石石雕·双龙戏珠
The Stone Carving of the Drum-shaped Doorframe
Bearing Stone of the Entrance of the Lower Ward:
Double Dragon Playing a Pearl

下院大门抱鼓石侧面
Side View of the Drum-shaped Doorframe Bearing
Stone of the Entrance of the Lower Ward

下院大门抱鼓石石雕·铺首衔环
The Stone Carving of the Drum-shaped Doorframe
Bearing Stone of the Entrance of the Lower Ward:
Animal Mask Holding a Ring in the Mouth

On the two sides of the doorway are two finely engraved drum-shaped doorframe-bearing stones. On the drumheads of the doorframe-bearing stones, the "double dragon playing a pearl" surrounded by a ring of "endless rich and high-ranking (pearl roundel)" designs are carved, the pad is decorated by the *kui*-unipedal dragon design and the base is "carried by the golden monkey", all of which had the meanings of getting rid of evil beings and protect the residences. The side walls of the entrance all are decorated with "book" designs, hinting that this was a literary family. In addition, the Lower Ward was also the location of the private school, so it was also called "the study yard". The inside lintel of the entrance was supported by the sparrow brackets, the lintels and block-and-bracket sets are all painted with color designs, the brick carvings on the front of the gables, such as the "peony flower" and the "Two Bats (Symbol of Good Fortune) Flanking a Character *Shou* (Longevity)", are all depicted vividly.

下院内，正面三孔窑洞是管家居住的，两侧的六孔厢窑有的作塾房，有的供佣人居住，北侧有一小圆门，是方便各院相互通连行走的阶梯暗道，也是佣人行走和小少爷们读私塾的通道。院门旁连接倒坐的以石板铺顶的马棚和放置草料的小房，内敞外扩，槽壁内长年被马匹磨损的痕迹依然可见。这里有个小小的故事——有一天，老石匠凿制马槽的时候，姜耀祖忽然来到他面前，用手中吸洋烟的铁钎子检验錾面工艺，结果与铁钎子的粗细标准略有相差，主人很生气，让老石匠重新返工打制。据说，这些马槽经三次打制才最终完成，可见主人对石雕工艺制作要求的严格。马槽底座墙壁上的拴马石锁也打制精细，安放得当。

下院马槽
The Stone Mangers in the Lower Ward

下院内景（由西南向东北摄）
The Internal Scene of the Lower Ward (SW-NE)

下院是陕北典型的"三三制"结构的"窑洞四合院"院落。其特点是宽大于深，敞亮、通风、纳阳极佳，给人以恢宏大气的感觉。"四合院"反映了"中规"、"中矩"、"天圆地方"、"天人合一"的建筑理念。窑洞从立面上看，是拱形，以一个圆心画弧而成，表现的是"中规"的"天"，而从平面上看，又是方形，表现的是"中矩"的"大地"。中规又中矩反映了古代中华民族对天象和地象的认识，人居于天地之间而成天、地、人的和谐共处，是古代人"天人合一"观念的具体反映和传承。

In the Lower Ward, the three stone-lined caves directly facing the entrance were the dorms of the steward, the six side caves flanking them were used as the classrooms of the private school or the dorms of the servants, , to the north of which is the stepped stone tunnel passage leading to the Middle and Upper Wards. On the inner side of the wall beside the entrance are the horse stables and fodder storehouses with stone plank roofs. On the stone mangers, the traces worn by the horses are still visible. For these mangers, there is also an anecdote: one day, when an old mason was working on chiseling a manger, Jiang Yaozu came to him and checked the quality of chiseling work with an iron rod for smoking opium and found that the size of the chiseled flutes did not match the thickness of the iron rod (which was exactly the size of the width of the chiseled flutes), he was very angry on this and ordered the old mason to make a new one. It is said that these mangers were renewed for three times to complete, showing the restrict standard of the owners to the stone carvings of the manor. The hitching holes on the base of the mangers are also carved carefully and arranged suitably.

The Lower Ward is the typical "cave quadrangle" courtyard of the "three-three" structure popular in northern Shaanxi. Its characteristics are the width is larger than the depth, spacious, well ventilated and sunlit, giving the visitors a feeling of magnificence and munificence. The "quadrangle courtyard" reflected the architectural designing ideas of "conforming to the compass (regular circle)", "conforming to the setsquare (rectangular)", "the circular heaven and the square earth" and "the harmony between the heaven and human". Seen from the elevation, the facade of the cave is a semicircular arch symbolizing the "heaven" which is "conforming to the compass (drawn circle)"; but seen from the plan, the cave dwelling is a rectangle symbolizing the "earth" which is "conforming to the setsquare (drawn square or rectangle)". These shapes reflected the understandings of ancient Chinese people to the universe: the harmonious coexistence of the human beings with the Heaven and Earth, between which they are living, is the concrete reflection and tradition of this idea.

下院屋脊（由东南向西北摄）
The Roof Ridges of the Lower Ward (SE-NW)

从下院的西侧经过石砌涵洞便可看到庄园的第二部分——中院。值得一提的是，庄园内的365个台阶，正合一年的天数，寓意一年四季，天天吉祥，岁岁平安，步步登高。

眼前这堵中院寨墙，高10米，长31米，整齐平展，伟岸壮观，宛如一扇巨大的屏风。这里有一个通往西南平台的门洞，洞门上方有"保障"二字石匾。这里也有一个传说——当年垒砌这堵寨墙时，一个中午，劳累了半天的工匠们在这荫凉的墙脚底下躺坐歇息，正在中院房内的姜耀祖忽然心神不宁，坐卧不安，急急走出大门大声催促："你们还在睡觉？快去上工！"就在工匠们离开墙脚的瞬间，墙体坍塌，滚石飞下，所幸工匠们无一所伤。惊魂未定的工匠们

连连说："是老天保佑，让姜老爷救了我们，天意！天意！"主人庆幸之余，重建寨墙时就特置"保障"二字。这"保障"二字还有更深刻的含义，与这堵寨墙的作用有着不可分割的关系。寨墙高于宅院一倍以上，面对大门，不是对外而是对内，被戏称为"反穿皮袄"。这种设计主要因为第一道入口的"大岳屏藩"寨墙是保卫宅院，主要起防守功能，而这第二道"保障"寨墙则起到"逃匿"和"反攻"的双重功能，寓意为"龙头"的后山炮台，易守难攻，镇守宅院，一旦各院失陷，则家人可穿"保障"寨门涵洞顺利转移至后山，届时寨门一关，守住寨头可控扼并反攻收复院落。所以，这是一种防卫—退却—反攻—收复环环相扣的防卫体系。

下院通往中院的涵洞
（由东南向西北摄）
The Tunnel Going to the Middle Ward from the Lower Ward (SE-NW)

中院寨墙（由北向南摄）
The Enclosure Wall of the Middle Ward (N-S)

Through the stone tunnel in the west of the Lower Ward, we are reaching the second part of the manor—the Middle Ward. It is worth mentioning that the three hundred and thirty-five steps in this manor exactly meet the number of the days in a year, which hints the hope of auspicious everyday, peaceful every year and upward every step.

This manor wall of the Middle Ward is ten meters high and thirty-one meters long; it is regular and straight like a huge screen. This tunnel leading to the southwest terrace has a stone board over its entrance, the inscription of which is "*Baozhang* (Safeguarding)". About this, there is also an anecdote: when this wall was built, the laborers who had worked for half a day were just resting in the shadow of this wall, Jiang Yaozu, who had been staying in the room,

suddenly felt uneasy, then got out of the room and urged the laborers: "are you still sleeping? Get up and go to work!" As soon as the laborers left the wall shadow, the wall collapsed and the stone blocks fell everywhere but the laborers. The laborers barely recovered from the fright said: "it is the God revealed Master Jiang to save us from the death! His urging is the revelation of the God!" To prevent this accident from happening again, Jiang Yaozu ordered to set this board with the inscription "*Baozhang*" inlayed on this wall. These two characters have even more profound connotations, which is inseparable from the function of this manor wall. This wall is two times as high as the courtyard and facing the gate, looking like guarding against the inside rather than the outside and has been joked as "wearing the fur with the hairs inside." This design is because the wall at the Lower Ward with the "*Da Yue Pingfan* (the safeguard of the Great Mountain)" board was built for defending the manor, but this second manor wall has double function of "escape" and "counterattack". The cannon battery on the hilltop behind the manor was the last stronghold for the manor, when the three wards were all captured by the attackers, the whole family could escape through this tunnel to the hilltop and close this door to hold the cannon battery. Therefore, this is a defense system integrated defending-retreating-counterattacking-recovering steps together.

中院全景（由西南向东北摄）
Full-view of the Middle Ward (SW-NE)

096

中院，坐东北向西南，门庭仍以水磨青砖的砖木结构砌筑，猫头滴水，五脊六兽硬山顶，脊饰"祥云瑞草"，墀头砖雕"福禄寿喜"、"天官赐福"、"麒麟送子"、"万象更新"、"缠枝牡丹"等图案，寓意福禄祯祥、子嗣兴旺、富贵不断。"凤凰戏牡丹"木雕雀替，额枋、"一斗四升麻叶头"彩绘斗拱，寓意柴米油盐。抱鼓石雕有"双狮捧面"、"麒麟吐书"等，并浮雕"福"、"寿"字样。侧壁砖廊镶嵌"福"、"寿"二字，富丽堂皇，庄重大气。门额镶嵌"武魁"匾，以彰显主人叔父姜鹰翔曾于道光二年（1822年）高中第十七名武举之荣耀。门簪又以"锤花"图案装饰，可以说是"装饰与教化相融，艺术与精神共存"。

中院院门（由西南向东北摄）
The Entrance of the Middle Ward (SW-NE)

中院院门门楼
（由西南向东北摄）
The Gateway of the Entrance of the
Middle Ward (SW-NE)

The Middle Ward, which is facing southwest, also has the entrance in the form of a house with gable roof built with gray bricks, the roof of which has five ridges and six roof figures; the ridge is decorated with auspicious cloud and felicitous plant designs, and the front of the gables are decorated with the brick carvings of "bat, deer, magpie and elder", "heavenly official bestowing good fortune", "a qilin delivering a child", "intertwined peony" and so on, symbolizing good fortune, high official position, happiness, longevity and high fertility. The wood carving "a phoenix playing peony flowers" of the sparrow brackets and lintels, and the bracket sets painted with color patterns hint the household supplies for daily use. The doorframe bearing stones have designs of "double lion holding a ball", "a qilin spitting out a jade letter", as well as characters "fu (good fortune)" and "shou (longevity)". The side walls of the entrance are also inlayed with these two characters. Over the doorway, a wooden board with the inscription "Wu Kui (Principal Graduate of the Imperial Military Examination)" is inlayed in memory of Jiang Yingxiang, the uncle of Jiang Yaozu, who has been graduated in the Imperial Military Examination as the seventeenth highest score in the second year of Daoguang Era (1822). The door pins on the door header are made into the shape of "lobed mace" to demonstrate this. It can be described as "the instruction is merged into the decorations, and the art coexists with the spirit."

中院全景（由西南向东北摄）
Full-view of the Middle Ward (SW-NE)

中院院门门楼外额（由西南向东北摄）
The Outer Lintel of the Gateway of the Entrance of the
Middle Ward (SW-NE)

中院院门门楼内额（由东北向西南摄）
The Inner Lintel of the Gate Tower of the Entrance of the Middle
Ward (NE-SW)

中院院门 "武魁" 木匾
The Wooden Board with Inscription *Wu Kui* (Principal
Graduate of the Imperial Military Examination)" over the
Entrance of the Middle Ward

中院院门斗拱彩绘
The Color-painting of the *Dougong*-bracket Sets of the
Entrance of the Middle Ward

中院院门墀头砖雕·麒麟送子
The Brick Carving of the Front of the Gable of the
Entrance of the Middle Ward: A Qilin Delivering a Child

中院院门墀头砖雕·福禄寿喜
The Brick Carving of the Front of the Gable of the Entrance of the Middle
Ward: Bat, Deer, Magpie and Elder (Symbolizing Good Fortune, High
Official Position, Happiness and Longevity)

中院院门墀头砖雕·天官赐福
The Brick Carving of the Front of the Gable of the Entrance of the Middle
Ward: the Heavenly Official Bestowing Good Fortune

中院院门墀头砖雕·狮子滚绣球
The Brick Carving of the Front of the Gable of the
Entrance of the Middle Ward: Lions Playing Colored
Silk Balls

中院院门墀头砖雕·石榴
The Brick Carving of the Front of the Gable of the
Entrance of the Middle Ward: Pomegranates

中院院门墀头砖雕·寿桃
The Brick Carving of the Front of the Gable of the
Entrance of the Middle Ward: Longevity Peaches

中院院门雀替木雕·凤凰戏牡丹
The Wood Carving of the Sparrow Bracket of the
Entrance of the Middle Ward: A Phoenix Playing
Peony Flowers

中院院门侧壁砖雕·蝴蝶流云
The Brick Carving of the Medallion of the
Side Wall of the Entrance of the Middle Ward:
Butterflies and Flying Clouds

中院院门侧壁和抱鼓石
The Side Wall and the Drum-shaped Doorframe Bearing
Stone of the Entrance of the Middle Ward

中院院门抱鼓石侧面
Side View of the Drum-shaped Doorframe Bearing Stone
of the Entrance of the Middle Ward

中院院门抱鼓石侧面
Side View of the Drum-shaped Doorframe Bearing Stone
of the Entrance of the Middle Ward

中院院门抱鼓石正面石雕·福寿双全
The Stone Carving on the Obverse of the Drum-shaped Doorframe Bearing Stone of the Entrance of the Middle Ward: Three
Bats Surrounding a Character "*Shou*" (Symbolizing the Possession of Both Good Fortune and Longevity)

中院院门柱杆石雕·绵绵瓜瓞
The Stone Carving of the Stone Pillar Base of the Entrance of the Middle Ward: Endlessly Intertwining Gourds and Vines
(Metaphor of Strong Fecundity)

中院院门山花砖雕·夏莲流云
The Brick Carving of the Gable of the Entrance of the
Middle Ward: Summer Lotus and Flying Cloud

中院影壁砖雕全景（由西南向
东北摄）
The Brick Carvings of the Screen Gate of
the Middle Ward (SW-NE)

中院影壁狩头
The Chishou (Ridge-end Beast) of the
Screen Gate of the Middle Ward

门内是水磨砖雕影壁"圆门"，外圆内方，寓意天圆地方。额饰砖雕"旭日东升"，寓意旭日普照，如日中天。拱眼壁饰砖雕"文王访贤"（周文王请姜太公出山辅佐西周）图案，主人自喻同姜太公一样，"怀才隐居"，一旦机遇到来，便可"出将入相"。另则，姜太公在此，也自然"百无禁忌，大吉大利"。内额拱眼壁饰砖雕"赤炼丹心"图，从表面来看，"炼丹"是求长生不老，实则表达主人怀有报效朝廷的一片丹心。额饰砖雕"福寿双全"，两边为"牡丹富贵"，"双龙戏珠"以祥云雕边衬托"棋琴书画"图案，寓意书香门第，情趣高雅。

At the center of the courtyard in the entrance is a screen gate in the shape of a short wall with a roof-shaped top and fine brick carving decorations. The outline of the screen is rectangular and the doorway is circular, hinting the old cosmic view of "the Heaven is circular and the Earth is square." The inter-bracket set boards of the obverse of the screen gate are decorated with the brick carving of the scenes of "King Wen (of the Western Zhou Dynasty) visiting the Sage (Grand Duke Jiang)", showing that the manor owner simulated himself as Grand Duke Jiang, who "hid himself from the society with unnoticed talents"; once the opportunity came, he could be "assigned as general out of the court and as prime minister in the court." In addition, because Grand Duke Jiang is here, "all taboos will be in abeyance, and everything is auspicious." The inter-bracket set boards of the reverse of the screen gate are decorated with the brick carving of the scenes of "A Taoist alchemist making golden elixir" which seems to show the pursuit of immorality but the real connotation is to reflect the loyalty of the master to the imperial court. The lintel of the screen gate is decorated with brick carvings of "Two bats flanking a character *shou* (symbolizing the possession of both good fortune and longevity)" flanked by "Peony flower" and "Double dragon playing a pearl" and "*weiqi*-go chess", "*qin*-zither", "books" and "painting scrolls" surrounded by margin of "auspicious cloud" patterns, hinting that the Jiang Family was an intellectual family with elegant tastes.

中院影壁（由西南向东北摄）
The Screen Gate of the Middle Ward (SW-NE)

中院影壁（由南向北摄）
The Screen Gate of the Middle Ward (S-N)

中院影壁砖雕·斗拱
The Brick Carving of the Screen Gate of the Middle
Ward: Dougong-bracket Set

中院影壁砖雕·旭日东升
The Brick Carving of the Screen Gate of the Middle
Ward: Sunrise

中院影壁砖雕·文王访贤
The Brick Carving of the Screen Gate of the Middle Ward: King Wen (of
the Western Zhou Dynasty) Visiting the Sage

中院影壁砖雕·文王访贤
The Brick Carving of the Screen Gate of the Middle Ward: King Wen (of the
Western Zhou Dynasty) Visiting the Sage

中院影壁砖雕·棋
The Brick Carving of the Screen Gate of the
Middle Ward: *Weiqi* (Go-chess)

中院影壁砖雕·琴
The Brick Carving of the Screen Gate of the
Middle Ward: *Qin*-zither

中院影壁砖雕·书
The Brick Carving of the Screen Gate of the
Middle Ward: Books

中院影壁砖雕·画
The Brick Carving of the Screen Gate of the
Middle Ward: Painting Scrolls

中院影壁砖雕·赤炼丹心
The Brick Carving of the Screen Gate of the Middle Ward: A Taoist Alchemist Making Golden Elixir

中院影壁砖雕·福寿双全
The Brick Carving of the Screen Gate of the Middle Ward: Two Bats Flanking a Character
Shou (Symbolizing the Possession of Both Good Fortune and Longevity)

中院影壁砖雕·双龙戏珠
The Brick Carving of the Screen Gate of the Middle Ward: Double Dragon Playing a Pearl

中院影壁和马棚（由东北向西南摄）
The Screen Gate and Horse Stables of the Middle Ward (NE-SW)

中院是以厢房式结构的"四合院"院落,石板铺地,宽敞明亮,两侧的三间大厢房,附小耳房,是主人接待宾客和社交往来的场所。正面的两孔小圆窑相当于现在的接待办公室,负责客人的饮食起居等事宜。贵客接待于东厢房,次之接待于西厢房。东厢房比西厢房稍高 0.2 米,这微小的尺度变化在庞大的宅群中并不明显,为什么这样建造呢?这是按照古代"昭穆之制"——左为尊位、东为上位的习俗而建,是帝王思想的反映和等级制度的体现,符合东大西小的民俗格式。再请大家看看左右厢房上横梁外端分别撰写的是"福禄"、"祯祥"和"整洁"、"长发",可谓"求工于一笔之内,寄情于点画之间"。这里有令人称道

The Middle Ward is a courtyard enclosed by rooms and paved with square stone boards, spacious and bright. It is flanked by a side room with three bays and an attached wing room on each side, which are the places for receiving guests. The side rooms are used as present-day reception office in charge of the lodging and living of the guests. The distinguished guests were received in the east side room and the common guests were received in the west side room. It is almost unnoticeable that the east side room is 0.2 m higher than the west side room; this arrangement is the remnant of the ancient *zhaomu* system that regarding the left side as the superior side and the east side is the upper side, reflecting the local custom

中院西厢房和耳房
（由东南向西北摄）
West Side and Wing Rooms of the Middle Ward (SE-NW)

中院东厢房和耳房
（由西北向东南摄）
East Side and Wing Rooms of the Middle Ward (NW-SE)

的砖、木、石三雕艺术的结合。西耳房上边的这一幅"万世基业"图窗棂，中间是卍（万）字的符号结构，周边镶嵌四片柿叶，既有万（卍）事如意的寓意，又蕴含事业（柿叶）发达的愿望。中间这一幅是"步步锦"图，窗棂结构以小到大、从内到外逐渐扩大，寓意家业日益昌盛，锦上添花。下面这一幅是变形"寿"字图案，美观大方。就连这室内的门墩也以"瓜"的

图形来装饰，寓意绵绵瓜瓞、子嗣兴旺。这里的墀头砖雕甚为讲究，这幅以猫、蝴蝶和梅花组成的"耄耋遐寿"图，雕刻十分精细。"猫"、"蝶"是谐音，指耄耋老人，就是八九十岁的老人，梅花斗霜傲雪，象征着老人像寒梅一样坚韧不拔的品格，又包含了晚辈祝福长辈长寿的一片忠孝之心。中间的这幅"喜报三元"图栩栩如生，以喜鹊和三个桂圆组成。喜鹊寓

and the hierarchical system. Let's see the outer ends of the beams of the side rooms, which have the characters of "*fulu* (good fortune and high official rank)", "*zhenxiang* (auspicious)" and "*zhengjie* (orderly and clean)", "*changfa* (sustainable developing)", every detail of which are depicted cautiously and carrying the feelings of the master. We can see the assemblage of the arts of the brick, wood and stone carvings in this courtyard. The top section of the window grills of the west wing room is the design of "Enterprise for thousands of generations", which is a swastika sign in the center and four persimmon leaves are inlayed around it; the swastika is the

symbol of "everything goes at will", and the pronunciation of the persimmon leaf in Chinese (*shiye*) is the same as that of "enterprise", the combination of which meant "the enterprise develops at will". The middle section of the window grills of this room is the design of "*Bubujin*", which consists of the lattice in nesting rectangular patterns expanding from the center outward, symbolizing the daily prospering family. The bottom one is a stylized design of a character *shou* (longevity), which is simple but elegant. The pillar bases are also decorated with the design of "Endlessly intertwining gourds and vines", which is the metaphor of strong fecundity and flourishing descendants.

中院东厢房窗棂木雕·步步锦
The Wood Carving of the Window Grill of the East Side Room of the Middle Ward: Bubujin (Lattice in Nesting Rectangular Pattern, Symbolizing Booming Everyday)

中院西耳房窗棂木雕·万世基业
The Wood Carving of the Window Grill of the West Wing Room of the Middle Ward: Swastika Surrounded by Four Persimmon Leaves (Metaphor of "Enterprise for Thousands of Generations")

中院西耳房窗棂木雕·"寿"字
The Wood Carving of the Window Grill of the West Wing Room of the Middle Ward: the Character *Shou* (Longevity)

The brick carvings of the front of the gables of this ward are very elaborate: this motif of "Longevity" composed of a cat, a butterfly and plum blossoms is carved very carefully and closely. The "cat" and "butterfly" in Chinese are homophones of "octogenarian and nonagenarian", reflecting the wish of longevity of the youths to the elders. This "Getting number one successively in three levels of the Imperial Examinations (a magpie and three longans)" is carved vividly; the magpie is the messenger of happy news, and the pronunciation of three longans in Chinese are the same as "three number ones", which are the highest achievements in the three levels of the Imperial Examinations, hinting the eager hopes of getting great merits of the elders to the youths. This scene of "Lotus flower and egret" on the top seems to express the fine spirit of "unstained from the filth" but the more profound connotation is that the lotus flower has the "feminine" nature and the egret has the "masculine" nature; the joining of these two natures can make endless lives.

Now let us see the scene of "A mouse eating grapes" in the middle of the front of the gable of the east side room. We

中院东耳房亮窗砖雕·蝙蝠流云
The Brick Carving of the Rear Window of the East Wing Room of the Middle Ward: Bats and Flying Clouds

中院西耳房墀头砖雕·耄耋遐寿
The Brick Carving of the Front of the Gable of the West Wing Room of the Middle Ward: A Cat Pursuing a Butterfly Under Plum Blossoms (Metaphor of Longevity)

意喜事盈门，三个桂圆谐音"三元"，含解元、会元、状元之喻，是长辈期盼晚辈高中功名的殷切寄托。上面的这幅"荷花鹭鸶"图，从表面上看，是表达主人出淤泥而不染的一种高雅心境，而其更深刻的含义是，荷花为"阴"，鹭鸶为"阳"，阴阳结合，生生不息。

再看东厢房——墀头中间的这幅"鼠食葡萄"图亦有深意。大家知道，鼠乃属相之首，子鼠为先，包含"大"和"尊"的意思。葡萄为紫色，厢房为东，寓意"紫气东来"。上面的这幅"福在眼前"图，两边是蝙蝠展翅，谐音"福"，中间是一枚"光绪通宝"铜钱，从"钱眼"穿过一条丝线，谐音"眼前"，寓意贵客临门，享有无尽的福气和财运。我们也祝愿朋友们，一年四季，福气多多，财源滚滚，事业有成！

这里的每一款匾刻都有讲究，或阐述一个道理，或显现一种心境，或祝愿金榜题名，或颂扬忠孝双全。这无处不在、无处不精的砖、木、石三雕艺术，充分反映出黄土文化的外在与内涵，以及一方民众的聪明才智、鉴赏品味和文化意识。

中院西厢房墀头砖雕·喜报三元
The Brick Carving of the Front of the Gable of the West Side Room of the Middle Ward: A Magpie and Three Longans (Metaphor of Getting Number One Successively in Three Levels of the Imperial Examinations)

中院西厢房墀头砖雕·荷花鹭鸶
The Brick Carving of the Front of the Gable of the West Side Room of the Middle Ward: Lotus Flower and Egret

know that in the twelve zodiac animals, the mouse is the first, which has the connotations of "large" and "superior". The color of the grapes is purple, so the image of grapes on the east side room hints the "purple air (the nimbus of a sage) comes from the east". The motif of "Good fortune before the eye" on the top is composed of two bats flanking a bronze *Guangxu tongbao* coin with its square hole gone through by a silk thread; the name of "bat" is pronounced the same as the "good fortune", and the hole of the coin symbolizes the situation of "before the eye", so their combination is the metaphor that good fortune and wealth are coming soon. Hereby I also hope our friends have good fortune day by day and year by year!

Every inscription and every board in this manor has its intention and meaning; or to explain a principle, or to express a feeling, or to make a wish, or to admire a virtue. The brick, wood and stone carving artworks displayed everywhere in this manor thoroughly reflect the appearance and connotation of the Loess Culture and the intelligence, connoisseurship and cultural tastes.

中院东厢房墀头砖雕·鼠食葡萄
The Brick Carving of the Front of the Gable of the East Side Room of the Middle Ward: Mouse Eating Grapes (Metaphor of Flourishing Descendants)

中院东厢房墀头砖雕·福在眼前
The Brick Carving of the Front of the Gable of the East Side Room of the Middle Ward: Bats Flanking the Coin with Square Hole (Metaphor of Good Fortune Before the Eye)

中院内景（由南向北摄）
The Internal Scene of the Middle Ward (S-N)

中院屋脊（由西南向东北摄）
The Roof Ridges of the Middle Ward (SW-NE)

我们再穿过这个过道去看东仓窑——窑高 5 米，宽 4.7 米，进深 14 米（俗称"枕头窑"）。东西两个仓窑内各设有 12 个大石仓和坐于仓顶的小石仓，每仓储粮 50 余石，每石以 60 公斤计算，共可储粮 7 万余公斤（1200 余石）。据说，当时主人的土地范围已扩大和延伸到毗邻的绥德、佳县等县，可见其范围之大、分布之广、储粮之多。碑文记载，清光绪二十六年（1900 年），"绥米岁凶，哀魂遍野，公输粮散，赈济灾民，实为仁泽，被民众称颂也"。我们从这段记载中可以看出，姜耀祖急民众之危难，救乡邻于水火，慈悲为怀，乐善好施，令人敬佩。

请大家稍微放松一下，站在这里可以领略周边的黄土风貌。这里属于典型的陕北农耕区域，有着浓厚的黄土风情和文化底蕴，正是这样的水土风情，孕育

中院东仓窑粮仓
The Internal Scene of the Eastern Barn Cave in the Middle Ward

中院东仓窑和葡萄院
（由西向东摄）
The Eastern Barn Cave and Grape Yard in the Middle Ward (W-E)

和造就了一方民众的习俗和品格。

　　大家再随我到西院。这里也叫碾磨院。上是西仓窑，下为碾磨房，这几个留在墙壁上的小石洞是碾米磨面时用于搭建帐篷的插孔。下面的这个小圆窑是放置筛米箩面用具的地方。中间这一孔小圆窑，我想大家是猜不到的。当年，朝廷腐败，兵荒马乱，民不聊生，时有盗贼抢劫和匪徒出没，主人为了防范外来侵袭的威胁，特挖造了这个以窑洞作掩饰的暗道（即窨子）。暗道纵深 200 余米直通后山，洞内弯曲，多处设障，如遇特大危急时可以藏身或脱险。由此可以看出，庄园虽有威严高耸的寨墙和壁垒森严的寨门，主人仍有防患于未然的自我保护意识。

中院西仓窑、碾磨院和地道
（由南向北摄）

The Western Barn Cave, Mill Courtyard and
Tunnel in the Middle Ward (S-N)

Through this narrow passage, we are going to the Eastern Barn Cave, which is five meters high, 4.7 meters wide and 14 meters deep, and it is called as "big pillow cave" by local people. It has 12 large stone barns and small stone barns over them, each set of the barns could store over fifty *shi* of grains, and the two barn caves could store over 1200 *shi* of grains, or more than 70 tons. It is said that the farmlands owned by the Jiang Family were extended as far as the Suide and Jiaxian Counties at that time. As recorded by the tablet inscription, in the twenty-sixth year of Guangxu Era of the Qing Dynasty (1900), "famine attacked Suide and Mizhi Counties, the dead bodies of starve were lying everywhere in the land, the Master (Jiang Yaozu) dispersed the grains from his barns to relief the hungry people, and this benefit was appreciated by the people." From this record, we know that Jiang Yaozu was such a generous gentleman and liked to help the people in hard times, which is really admirable.

Now we can have a break here to enjoy the loess landscape around the manor. The environment here belongs to the typical agricultural area of northern Shaanxi with thick loess folklore and cultural connotation, bred and cultivated the custom and nature of the people living in this area.

Please follow me to the western courtyard, which is also called mill courtyard. Up there is the Western Barn Cave, and down here is the mill. These stone holes are used to erect canopy when the grains were processed in this yard. This small round cave is the cellar to store coarse and fine sieves and other utensils for processing grains. This small round cave in the middle, I guess you cannot guess its usage. At that time, the government was corrupt and the society was in turmoil, robbers and bandits were usually harassing the people. To guard against and escape from the attacks by them, the owners of this manor dug this escape tunnel camouflaged by a cave dwelling. This tunnel, which is over 200 meters long, goes all the way to the rear hill, and it has many turns and defense works, the residents in this manor could shelter or escape from the danger. These facilities show us that although this manor was protected by the high walls and firm castles, the owners still had strong self-caution conscience.

中院外鸡鸭院（由东北向西南摄）
The Poultry Stables Outside the Middle Ward (NE-SW)

中院通往下院的阶梯暗道
The Stepped Secret Passage Linking the Middle and the Lower Wards

我们再沿着 15 个垂带踏垛而上便可看到庄园的第三部分——上院。

上院是主人居住的院落，也是整个庄园的主体建筑。院门为筒瓦卷棚式砖木结构，垂花门柱举架，额枋、荷墩彩绘，"富贵"雀替，牡丹、夏莲雕空花板。门额镶嵌"武魁"匾，九世祖姜怀德（姜耀祖的曾祖父）亦中武举以此纪念。两侧的方形石雕门墩上卧浮雕"狮子滚绣球"，侧雕鹤、鹿、松、竹、夏莲、牡丹，争芳斗妍。门楼两侧各设神龛，敬祀天地神位。廊心墙砖雕"鹿奔松林"、"鹤唳寿石"、"日月相映"，它以"鹿鹤"之谐音，寄意于东、西、南、北、上、下之"六合"，合称"鹿鹤同春"，寓意国泰民安、社会稳定、日月生辉、福寿无疆。绿色门扇镶有铜制铺首衔环、流云踢角，30 个五路泡钉依次排列，既对门心板起到牢固连接作用，又在外观上显出庄严气势。圆鼓形基石柱木顶立的屏风门与大门连为一体，整座门楼高大气派。按照传统习俗，此屏风门在婚丧嫁娶、接待贵客时才可以打开。东西两端分设小圆门，西去厕所，东下塾院。门内额题"安乐居"三字，窑面写有"忠正和平"、"安居光泽"，表达主人安居乐业、忠厚正派、福泽子孙的期盼和愿望。

上院院门（由西南向东北摄）
The Entrance of the Upper Ward (SW-NE)

Going upward along the fifteen steps, we are going to the third part of the manor—the Upper Ward.

The Upper Ward is the residence of the master of the manor. The entrance of the ward is a festooned gate with arched roof ridge built of brick and timber, the beams, pillars, doorframe and roof truss are all painted with color decorations. Over the lintel of the entrance, a wooden board with inscription "*Wu Kui* (principal graduate of the Imperial Military Examination)" is inlayed, which is in memory of Jiang Huaide (the ninth generation of Jiang Family and great-grandfather of Jiang Yaozu) who has graduated in the Imperial Military

上院院门（由东向西摄）
The Entrance of the Upper Ward (E-W)

上院内景（由南向北摄）
The Internal Scene of the Upper Ward (S-N)

上院全景（由南向北摄）
Full-view of the Upper Ward (S-N)

Examination. The square doorframe-bearing stones beside the entrance are decorated with the carvings of "Lions playing a colored silk ball", crane, deer, pine tree, bamboos, summer lotus, peony, and so on. On the walls beside the entrance, shrines are set to worship the deities of the heaven and soil. The porch end walls of the entrance are decorated with brick carvings of "Deer running in the pine forest", "Crane crowing in the bamboo grove" and "the sun and moon shining together"; in Chinese, the pronunciation of "deer and crane" is similar to that of "the six directions (east, west, south, north, heaven, earth)", expressing the with for the peaceful and prosperous nation, stable society and endless good fortune and longevity. The green lacquered

上院垂花门局部
The Hanging-flower Gate of the Upper Ward (Detail)

上院垂花门局部
The Hanging-flower Gate of the Upper Ward (Detail)

door leaves have bronze *pushou*-doorknockers, capped nails and cloud-shaped margin fittings. The thirty capped nails arranged in five rows not only reinforced the door leaf panels but also showed the lofty manner. Inside the entrance, another screen gate built on drum-shaped stone plinths is linked to the entrance. According to the traditional custom, this screen gate was only opened in the occasions of important events, such as wedding or funeral ceremonies or the reception of distinguished guests. On the east and west ends of the inner enclosure wall of the Upper Ward, there are small doorways: the east one leads to the Middle and Lower Wards and the west one leads to the restroom. On the lintel of the inner side of the entrance, the board with inscription "*Anle Ju* (Cozy Residence)" is hung, expressing the desire of the master for the peaceful life.

上院垂花门局部
The Hanging-flower Gate of the Upper Ward (Detail)

上院院门"武魁"木匾
The Wooden Board with Inscription "*Wu Kui* (Principal Graduate of the Imperial Military Examination)" over Gateway of the Upper Ward

上院垂花门荷墩彩绘
The Color-painted Lotus Flower-shaped Post Block of the Hanging-flower Gate of the Upper Ward

上院屏风门（由东北向西南摄）
The Screen Gate of the Upper Ward(NE-SW)

上院廊心墙砖雕·鹿奔松林

The Brick Carving of the Medallion of the Porch-end Wall of the
Upper Ward: Deer Running in the Pine Forest

上院廊心墙砖雕·鹤唳寿石

The Brick Carving of the Medallion of the Porch-end Wall of the
Upper Ward: Crane Crowing in the Bamboo Grove

上院院门西侧砖雕·神龛
The Brick Carving on the West Side of the Entrance
of the Upper Ward: Deity Shrine

上院院门门墩石雕·荷花鹭鸶
The Stone Carving of the Stone Base of the Entrance
of the Upper Ward: Lotus and Egret

上院院门门墩石雕·凤穿竹林、鹿鹤同春
The Stone Carving of the Stone Base of the Entrance of the Upper
Ward: Phoenix and Bamboo Forest, Deer and Crane (Metaphors
of High Official Position and Longevity)

上院院门门墩石雕·牡丹富贵、福寿延年
The Stone Carving of the Stone Base of the Entrance of the
Upper Ward: Peony Flowers, Phoenix, Deer and Character *Shou*

上院是陕北典型的"明五暗四六厢窑"式结构的窑洞院落。"明五"是指正面台阶上的这五孔石窑（称"上窑"），是主人居住的，它的含义是"五子登科"。主人夫妇居中，侧配分居两旁各室。"暗四"是指上窑两旁的套院，即主人的厨院和库房，俗称"暗四间"，它的含义是"四喜盈门"。"六厢窑"是指两侧的六孔窑洞，是晚辈居住的，它的含义是"六六大顺"。这"明五暗四六厢窑"合数为十五，从建筑理念来讲，无论是分是合，均取单数，单数是增，双数为圆，是期望人口增加、财产增值，隐含"人财两旺"的寓意。

院落修造豪华，铺设讲究，恢宏大气；窑内炕裙壁画，暖阁壁橱，水磨石灶；地面由菱形石板铺砌，落落大方。"枪头梅花格"木雕窗棂，匀称有度，疏

上院窗棂木雕·三交嵌牡丹
The Wood Carving of the Window Grill of the Upper
Ward: The Spearheads and Peony Flowers

上院窗棂木雕·枪头梅花格
The Wood Carving of the Window Grill of the Upper
Ward: The Spearheads and Plum Blossoms

密得体。枪、戟、戈、矛是古代兵器，喻以锐器进攻取胜；梅花斗霜傲雪，喻端庄美丽，又喻坚贞操守。阳刚之枪头和阴柔之梅花看似相左，实则代表"英雄"和"美人"两方。阴阳、雌雄在对立中统一，含文武双全、才子佳人之意，是圆满的意思。"三交嵌牡丹"图案，方圆互映，寓意富贵吉祥。盘长，也就是蛇抱九颗蛋，蛇象征男根，寓生殖能力强；而蛇又多产蛋，兆示人丁兴旺、子孙满堂。这实为生育文化的反映。以变形"寿"字而做的木格亮窗，辅以"双龙戏珠"、"龙头"门楣，以及这"万字格"、"丁字格"、"工字格"、"丹字格"、"三交格"、"如意格"等雕镂窗棂图案，典雅别致。檐头穿廊挑石，相当气派。

上院窗棂木雕·"寿"字
The Wood Carving of the Window Grill of the Upper Ward: The Character "*Shou* (Longevity)"

上院窗棂木雕·盘长
The Wood Carving of the Window Grill of the Upper Ward: Endless Knot (Chinese Knot)

The plan of the Upper Ward of the Jiang Family Manor is the typical pattern of "Five Main, Four Hidden and Six Side (Caves)" in the domestic architecture of the northern Shaanxi. The "Five Main" refers to the five main caves on the stone platform in the façade of the ward (which were called the "superior caves" and resided by the master of the household), the number "five" of which is the metaphor of "all of the sons (descendants) are going to get high official ranks". The "Four Hidden" refers to the caves in the kitchen courtyard (eastern yard) and warehouse courtyard (western yard), each of which has two, and the number "four" is the metaphor of "four happy events come together". The "Six Side" refers to the six side caves on the two sides of the courtyard, which were resided by the juniors, and the connotation of the number "six" is "everything goes well." The designing idea of this type of architectural complex is hoping the increasing of the population and the improving of the wealth and property.

The Upper Ward is built and decorated in a luxurious and exquisite manner: the main caves all have *kang* (heatable brick beds) and wall closets, the hearths are decorated with terrazzo and the floors are paved with rhombic stone planks. The window grill made into the wood carving design of "Spearheads and plum blossoms" is in a suitable spacing; the spearheads symbolize the endeavor for victory and the plum blossoms symbolize the graceful beauty and sturdy faith. The spearheads with masculine nature and the plum blossoms with feminine nature combined together show a harmonious marriage. The design of "Spearheads and peony flowers" symbolizes the hope of rich and lucky. The design of "*Panchang* (Chinese knot)" is actually a stylized woven snake holding nine eggs; the snake is a metaphor of strong fertility and the nine eggs hint the flourishing descendants, which can be seen as the reflection of the fertility culture. The sashes with the grills made into the stylized character

上院户门木雕
The Wood Carving of the Door of the Upper Ward

上院屋檐穿廊挑石
The Stone Cantilevers of the Porch Eave of the
Upper Ward

"*shou* (longevity)", the door lintels decorated with "double dragon playing a pearl" and "dragon head" designs, and the windows with grills made into swastika, T-shaped pattern, H-shaped pattern and other various patterns are all unique and exquisite. The eave supported by the stone cantilevers is stretched rather long into a porch, this is a reflection of economic strength.

大家来看围墙上的这个小方窗，它是方便主人传话的一个窗口，功能相当于现代的电话。还有这些留有石洞的大小石墩，每当主人需要张灯结彩，或者举办大型活动时，便可移动石墩，用来搭建帐篷。院中的这张大石床更是别具景致。当年，主人在院中亲手栽植的两棵老槐树，枝繁叶茂，绿树成荫，无论是在烈日炎炎的中午，还是在繁星点点的夜晚，主人都可以在大石床上悠闲自得、安然惬意地乘凉休息。这个环绕石床底部的石槽起什么作用呢？到了晚上，将水倒入石槽内，以水隔离，可以防止虫、蝎的侵袭，相当于护城河，设计十分科学。2003 年，拍摄革命历史巨片《延安颂》，一代伟人毛泽东与周恩来正是在这张大石床上，铺开作战地图，运筹帷幄，指引了中国革命的航程。倘若当年的主人在世，也会感到十分荣幸和无比自豪。

上院围墙设置的传话窗口
The Message Transmission Window on the
Enclosure Wall of the Upper Ward

上院内的石凉床（由西向东摄）
The Stone Bed in the Upper Ward (W-E)

Let's see this small square window on the enclosure wall. It is a message transmission window, the function of which is the same as the telephone today. These stone drums with holes on them are used for the owners to erect tents or canopies in occasions of holidays, festivals or other large-scale events. This large stone bed is a unique facility in this ward. In the past years, the two pagoda trees personally planted by the master in this ward had luxuriant foliage and dropped thick shadows to this bed, so the master could rest on this stone bed relaxed at the hot high noon or in the starry night. What is the function of this stone trough surrounding the base of this stone bed? In the evening, pour water into this trough, the insects and scorpion could be blocked away by this "moat" from the master lying on the stone bed, and this design is very scientific. In the revolutionary historic TV serial *The Ode to Yan'an* taped in 2003, the two great revolutionary leaders Mao Zedong and Zhou Enlai were facing the map spread on this stone bed to discuss the plan of the revolutionary wars and guide the sail of Chinese Revolution. If the old master of this manor was alive, he would be very proud about this.

我们来看东院，又叫厨房院。门额上刻有"养廉"二字，是主张艰苦朴素、勤俭持家，反对浪费，遵循了儒家学说的治家之道。大家随我进入院内，这个通往灶房的进水口和出水口，以鱼头鱼尾来装饰，设计新颖、美观实用，寓意鱼水相连，年年有余。背墙上的这个小圆窑是储藏食品的冷藏室，相当于今日的冰箱，具有较高的研究价值。院中的这个大石仓是储水的备用水仓。大石床是放置东西用的，到了夏天，主人还可以作为餐桌来乘凉吃饭。大家随我进入窑内，这孔窑洞是厨师居住的（俗称前后窑），穿过门洞便是主人的厨房。这排乡土气息浓厚的大小厨灶和放置调味品的小石仓，可以想象当年主人丰衣足食、安居乐业的富裕生活。

上院厨房院门额题字"养廉"
The Lintel Board of the Kitchen Courtyard with Inscription "*Yang Lian* (Cultivating Honesty and Cleanness)"

上院厨房院（东院）
（由西北向东南摄）
The Kitchen Courtyard (Eastern Yard) in the Upper Ward (NW-SE)

Now let's come to the kitchen yard, or the eastern yard. The inscription on the lintel board reads *"Yang lian"*, which means cultivating the virtue of honesty and cleanness and preventing waste, following the Confucian principles of running a household. The water inlet and outlet of this kitchen are made into the shapes of fish head and tail are not only artistic but also practical, and have the metaphor of "having surplus every year". This small cave on the back wall is the cold closet to store food, just like our refrigerator today. This large stone tank in the center of the yard was the backup water tank of the kitchen. The large stone beds were for storing groceries, in the summer, they could also be used as dinner tables. This cave was the dorm of the cooks (also called as front-and-rear cave), via the doorway is the main kitchen. These line of cooking stoves in different sizes and small stone spice cellars reflect the peaceful and happy life of the owners of the manor.

上院厨房院石雕·鱼头、鱼尾
The Stone Carvings of the Kitchen Courtyard in the Upper Ward:
Fish Head and Fish Tail

上院厨房院石雕·鱼头
The Stone Carving of the Kitchen Courtyard in the Upper Ward: Fish Head

上院厨房院石雕·鱼尾
The Stone Carving of the Kitchen Courtyard in the Upper Ward: Fish Tail

上院厨房院冷藏室
The Cold Closet at the Kitchen Courtyard in the Upper Ward

上院厨房院石床和水仓
The Stone Bed and Water Caves at the Kitchen Courtyard in the Upper Ward

我们再到西院，又叫库房院。门额上刻有"讲让"二字，要求家人与人往来应讲究礼仪诚恳、互谦互让，包含了一种儒家观念。这两孔窑内都有石仓，是存放米面的库房。套有的这个小圆窑，是主人冬季放置花卉和鸟笼的地方，可见主人还有戏玩鸟儿、养花种草的闲情逸致。再看门墩上的这四个石狮子，这里也有一个传说——当年一位老石匠制作出门墩石狮，姜耀祖看后觉得不够精巧，便打算另请高手雕制，结果请来的两个石匠看到石狮子后大为赞叹，对姜耀祖说："老师傅做不了的，我们就更做不了啦。"姜耀祖便仍然请回那位老石匠制作。因此，这四个石狮子依旧出自那位老石匠之手。由此可见，姜耀祖对石雕工艺的鉴赏要求是相当高的。请大家再随我观赏一个别有洞天的厢窑。这孔窑内阳光明媚，舒适安静，是主人吸洋烟的地方，放置精致的烟枪、灯具，供老爷、少爷们吸食鸦片，消磨岁月。据说，主人每年要吸掉几十石小米的烟土，这个烟枪究竟烧掉了多少银两，我们是无法计算的。而这也充分反映了当时地主阶级的奢侈堕落生活，鸦片不仅使姜氏家业年耗谷米几十余石，而且将几辈人的创业奋发精神消磨殆尽。可以说，

上院库房院（西院）
（由东南向西北摄）
The Warehouse Courtyard (Western Yard)
in the Upper Ward (SE-NW)

上院库房院门额题字"讲让"
The Inscription "*Jiang Rang*
(Advocating Courtesy)" on the Lintel Board of
the Warehouse Courtyard in the Upper Ward

Then we go to the warehouse yard, or the western yard. The inscription on the lintel board reads "*Jiang rang*", which means advocating courtesy, showing a kind of Confucian view. In these two caves, stone barns were built to store grains. This small round cave was for the master to store flowers and bird cage in the winter, and reflected his hobbies. These four stone lions on the doorframe bearing stone also have an anecdote. It is said that when these lions were just finished by an old mason, Jiang Yaozu thought that they were not elaborate enough, and sought for more skillful masons to carve a new set. How, two new masons admired these four stone lions when they saw them and said, "if the works of the old master cannot satisfy you, we would do even worse." Jiang Yaozu had to ask that old mason to go on his work. Therefore, these four stone lions we see today are still the artworks of that old mason. But this anecdote told us that Jiang Yaozu had very high connoisseurship on the stone carving art and his requirement to the quality of the stone carving artworks was rather high. This side cave is in a shiny and quiet position, and it was the location of the master to smoke opium. The exquisite opium pipes and smoke lamps set here were used by the owners of the manor to enjoy the drug and kill time. It is said that

姜氏后来的家道衰败与这种沉溺享乐、不思进取有直接的关系。

人生五光十色，生活丰富多彩。主人在养花种草，戏玩鸟儿的同时，尤其讲究个人卫生，这个过洞便是浴室，特制的石槽作为浴盆，这个石墩是沐浴之余喘息的坐处。请大家再随我观赏一个百余年前的"三星级"卫生间——上至帝王将相，下到平民百姓，有吃住便有拉撒。姜氏主人的这个厕所也同样讲究舒适。这把用榆木打制的坐式便椅，靠背刻有"寿"字图案，扶手圆滑，坐板挖孔，粪坑沉降于下层，右侧留有小

便石槽。坐在这通风透气的便椅上，既能自得其所，又可观望对面的无限风光，很是舒适。厕所总体设计，既方便又卫生，这虽比不上今天的抽水马桶，但在当时是相当超前的，就连山西晋商豪宅中也不多见。

各位朋友，各位游客，当我们的参观将要结束时，我向大家介绍一下姜氏创业发家的来历。

姜氏发家，始于姜耀祖的祖父姜安邦。姜安邦年轻时曾给杨家沟的地主马良打工，他为人忠厚，聪明能干，深得马良夫妇的赏识。马良便将女儿许配予他，并将常年索要不回的旧账和地租归他所有。姜安邦秉

上院吸洋烟的小窑
The Small Cave in the Upper
Ward for Smoking Opium

上院内的浴盆
The Bathtub in the Upper Ward

opium worth several dozens of *shi* of millet would be consumed by the Jiang Family Manor each year; how many silver dollars have been burnt away by this opium pipe, we have no idea to calculate. This setting shows us the luxurious and corrupt life of the landlord class at that time. Smoking opium spent not only the money and crop of the Jiang Family but also the creative and endeavoring spirits of the generations of their ancestors. We can say that the declining of the Jiang Family in later times is directly related to the indulging to the pleasure and addicting to the drugs of the successors.

The lives are diversified and the interests of the owners of this manor were also rich and varied. The master of the manor was very careful on the personal hygiene; this cave is the bathroom and this stone basin is his bathtub, and this stone stool is for resting after the bathing. Here is a "three-star" toilet built over one hundred years ago; it is also designed and built in an elegant and comfortable style. This commode chair made of elm wood has a character "*shou* (longevity)" on the back and is made in a suitable shape for the user to be seated at ease while enjoying the scenery outside.

It is not as good as the present-day flush toilet but at that time, it was rather advanced, and even very rare in the mansions of the famous *Jin* Merchants in Shanxi Province.

My dear friends, when we are finishing our visit, please let me introduce the history of the development of the enterprise of the Jiang Family.

The flourishing of the Jiang Family was started by Jiang Anbang, who is Jiang Yaozu's grandfather. When Jiang Anbang was young, he was employed by Ma Liang, a landlord at Yangjiagou Village, where Ma appreciated his loyalty, honesty and intelligence and married his daughter to Jiang Anbang, and transferred the loans and land rents to be returned and paid by the borrowers and tenants in the future to him. Since then, Jiang Anbang accumulated the first capital, and opened a shop named "Chongde (Admiring Virtue)" at Gezhendian Town (present-day Jizhen Town, Suide County, belonged to Mizhi County at that time). Just at this time, Ma Liang died of illness, and his son who named Ma Jiale held the wedding ceremony for his sister and Jiang Anbang.

性刚毅，才智过人，竟将所有的欠账全部收回。待他小有资本后，在圪针店（当时属米脂今绥德吉镇）开商铺"崇德号"做买卖，此时，马良不幸病故，由操持家务的马嘉乐主持为妹妹与姜安邦完婚。

姜安邦善于审时度势，据说，他还做过贩卖软米、砂锅和棺木的生意。清道光二年（1822年），陕北遭遇瘟疫，人们用砂锅熬中药，做"纸火盆"，死人安葬得做棺木，"过事"要吃软米糕。所以，砂锅、软米、棺木价格暴涨。姜安邦不断往返于米脂和圪针店之间做这挣钱的生意，财源广进，成了当地的首富。姜安邦娶妻四房，生有四子，前三子早年即逝，其大部分家业自然留于四子姜锦堂。姜锦堂娶妻四室，生有姜耀祖一子。姜锦堂54岁时便打算新修宅院，选址牛家梁山湾作为庄基地，于同治十年（1871年）破土兴工。因姜锦堂年老体衰，不胜操劳，便将许多监修事项交由12岁的姜耀祖掌管料理。光绪四年（1878年），姜锦堂去世，19岁的姜耀祖继续完成宅院的修建工程，并于光绪十二年（1886年）孟冬竣工落成。

姜耀祖为人性情直爽豪放，在建筑方面颇有建树。碑文记载："建筑自动工以至竣工约十五六年，宅分上中下三层，一切布置都由公独出心裁，其规模之宽敞新颖，吾陕北所仅有，所谓博大精神，与众不同也。"我们从姜氏家史和碑文记载可知，这座耗资巨大、用工无数、经16年漫长时间而建成的窑洞庄园，凝聚了主人和工匠们的智慧和血汗。

大家随我穿过"保障"门通道登上院落西南平台，一览庄园的整体布局和高原风貌。

站在这里，远眺逶迤起伏的红花岭山峦，俯视环绕牛家梁山下流淌的小河，我们就会看到，这里是地景学，也就是我们所说的"风水"的理想之地。"宁眠弯弓水，不居背弓溪"，山下有小溪襟带而过，这正是一处民间极为讲究的风水宝地。老子在《道德经》上讲，"万物负阴而抱阳，冲气以为和"。庄园正是坐落在牛家梁山湾三面环山的怀抱中，靠山深厚稳重，面向东南开口，恰似一个硕大的元宝，或者像一头金牛卧在山窝里，符合"负阴抱阳"的风水理念。而更为巧妙的是，主人因地制宜，根据山形地貌，运用园林理论中"步异景移"、"峰回路转"的构图手法，分别将底层的下院建造为坐西北向东南，而中院和上院则坐东北向西南，使各院都能争得良好的空间和方位，获得充足的日照，两相得宜，是聚财纳福、人财两旺的理想形胜。

陕北，是一块神奇的土地，历史上长期华夷杂居，中原文化与各民族文化相互融合，形成了这一特有的区域文化，这部屹立在黄土高原上的浓缩建筑景观，则是陕北黄土文化的真实写照。近半个世纪以来，数十部影视剧目在这里拍摄完成，成为展现黄土民俗风情的影视拍摄基地。2001年6月10日，中央电视台《东方时空·直播时刻》栏目，以姜氏庄园为专题向全球做了直播报道，真实地介绍了这座窑洞庄园的外在与内涵。这座历经了三代风云变幻的百年庄园，至今不减其迷人的魅力。俯瞰建筑群落，品味黄土地民俗风情，愿高原深处这一"西北民居第一宅"——姜氏庄园，给大家留下深刻而美好的回忆。

谢谢大家，欢迎再次光临！

Jiang Anbang was good at judging the situation and seizing the opportunities; his business was mainly trading and selling broomcorn millet, casseroles and coffin boards. In the second year of Daoguang Era of the Qing Dynasty (1822), northern Shaanxi was attacked by a plague, by which many people were killed. To concoct herbal medicine and to sacrifice the dead, the people needed casseroles; to bury the dead, they needed coffins; to entertain the attendants of the funeral affairs, broomcorn millet cake was the main food. Therefore, the prices of these three merchandises were rapidly rising. Jiang Anpang earned huge money by this chance by trading these goods back and forth between the Mizhi County seat and Gezhandian Town and became the richest landlord in that place. He had four sons, but three of them died at very young ages, so he left most of his businesses, in which there were over 6000 *mu* (more than 400 hectares) of farmlands, as legacy to Jiang Jintang, who was his fourth son. Jiang Jintang had only one son, who was Jiang Yaozu. When he was 54 years old, Jiang Jintang planned to build a new dwelling and chose the hill slope at Niujialiang as the location of the new manor and broke the ground in the tenth year of Tongzhi Era (1871) of the Qing Dynasty when he was 54 years old. Because he was too old to carry out all of the affairs about the construction, he handed over many affairs to Jiang Yaozu who was only 12 years old at that time to manage and supervise. In the fourth year of Guangxu Era

(1878) of the Qing Dynasty, Jiang Jintang died at the age of 61. Since then, this heavy task was transferred to the hands of Jiang Yaozu, who was just 19 years old. In the tenth month of the twelfth year of Guangxu Era (1886), the new manor was finally completed.

Jiang Yaozu had innovative ideas on architecture. As recorded by the tablet inscription, "This engineering lasted for about fifteen or sixteen years since the groundbreaking to the completion; the manor consisted of the upper, middle and lower stories, and every detail was designed by the master (Jiang Yaozu); the magnificence and originality of this mansion are matchless in our northern Shaanxi; its spaciousness and elegance are different from that of any others." From the family archives and the tablet inscription, we know that this huge cave manor completed by a long time of 16 years was the condensation of the intelligence, blood and sweat of the master and hundreds of craftsmen and laborers.

Please follow me go to the southwest terrace of the manor via this tunnel named "*Baozhang* (safeguarding)" and have a full view of the entire manor and the scenery of the plateau.

Here, when we look at the undulating Honghualing (Red Flower Ridge) in the distance, and overview the flowing brook below the Niujialiang Hill, we can find that this is an ideal topography of the landscape, or the so-called "*fengshui*" in the folklore. "I would rather lie in

the open air in the embrace of the water (current) than live in the house built on the back of the bow (outside the arch-shaped river or brook)." The brook flowing below the hill, on which the manor is built, formed an auspicious terrain highly reputed by the local people. Laozi wrote in his *Daode Jing* that "all things leave behind them the *yin* (obscurity and cold) and go forward to embrace the *yang* (brightness and warm), while they are harmonized by the breath of vacancy." This manor is just embraced by the mountains in three directions, which give it stable backs; the opening toward the southeast is like a huge gold ingot or a gold ox squatting in the mountain col, matching the *fengshui* idea of "leaving the *yin* behind them and go forward to embrace the *yang*." The cleverer point is that the master designed the three stories of his manor according to the scene-composition method of "changing the scenes along with the moving steps" and "(arranging the) winding paths amidst the complex terrains" in the garden theory, which arranged the Lower Ward in the bottom story to face the southeast, and the Middle and Upper Wards to face the southwest, making all of the wards enjoy the best orientation and space to get enough sunshine.

The northern Shaanxi is a magic land; in the history, the Han people and the peoples of many other ethnic groups have long been living together here and the cultures from the Central Plains and the tribes from the northern steppes ran into each other and converged here and formed the unique regional culture. This architectural artwork standing on the Loess Plateau is an embodiment of the Loess Culture. In the recent half a century, dozens of movies and TV serials have chosen here as the scene to shoot, and the Jiang Family Manor has become the bases of the movie and TV play shooting reflecting the customs and folklores of the Loess Plateau. On June 10, 2001, the LiveShow column of the "Oriental Horizon" program of CCTV globally broadcasted the Jiang Family Manor and faithfully introduced the appearance and connotation of this cave manor. This manor witnessed the rapidly changing history of the three generations and over one century is still keeping its charm. I hope this "No. 1 of the domestic architecture in northwestern China" can give you a impressive and beautiful memory.

Thank you all, Welcome to come again!

庄园全景（由北向南摄）
Full-View of the Jiang Family Manor (N-S)

后 记

经过多年的精心筹划和认真审慎的编纂，《姜氏庄园》画册终于付梓了。这让我激动不已，也让我兴奋不已。细细看来这部画册，全是汗水浇出，尽为心血染成。

雄浑的陕北黄土高原，是生我育我的地方。我深爱着这里的山、这里的水和这里的人，也深爱着这里深厚的文化和古老的建筑艺术，我在我深爱的这块黄土地上工作和生活了四十多个春秋。20世纪70年代以来，我从事文化艺术工作，创作了一些文艺作品、诗词曲赋等，有的剧目被搬上舞台，深入城乡广为演唱，有的剧目参加省市文艺会演，多次获得创作奖励，有的作品在国家、省、市戏剧评选中入围、获奖，有的文章在报纸杂志上刊登发表。90年代初，我开始从事文物工作，有幸参与了"米脂妇女革命史迹展览"的资料收集、策划、设计、布展等活动，以及馆藏文物的分类与建档建卡、全县文物普查与征集和文化市场稽查的工作。

2003年，我调任姜氏庄园文物管理所。近年来，我们接待了不少国内外文物研究者、爱好者和采风摄影者，他们都企盼能看到一本全面介绍有关姜氏庄园的书籍。我在长期对姜氏庄园建筑价值与文化内涵的挖掘研究及资料收集、整理工作中，深感这一民居建筑的文化厚重与博大精深，于是便有了把这些珍贵资料编纂成册的想法。在诸多同仁、朋友们的关心、鼓励与支持下，我坚定了编纂画册的信心。

2006年5月开始，我即着手有关资料的整理与编纂工作。我与同仁们利用工作之余，身背照相机，骑上摩托车，跑坟茔、抄碑文、制拓片、查族谱、阅县志。寒来暑往，年复一年，在不同时节、不同位置、不同角度，用镜头记录和展示姜氏庄园一景一物的独特风貌。不舍寒冬，不辞酷署，伏案撰文，比照筛选。对每一篇文稿内容的翔实准确和每一张图片视觉的色彩效果，我又一次次地修改和一次次地拍摄，宵衣旰食，不辞辛劳，凡此种种，不一而足。有感于此，缘于"地近易核"之便，日积月累，殚精竭虑，而有所成。

经过多年大量调查、考证和研究，进一步深解细悟，整理完善，撰写了6万多字的文稿，精选出

Postscript

After years of painstaking planning and cautious compiling, this album *Jiang Family Manor* is going to be published. I am very glad and excited for the coming of this event.

I was born on the magnificent Loess Plateau in the northern Shaanxi and have lived here for over 40 years. I deeply love the land and people here, as well as the profound culture and architectural art. Since the 1970s, I have been engaged in the cultural and art causes and composed some literature works. In the early 1990s, I was assigned to work on the cultural relics post.

In 2003, I was transferred to work in the commission for preservation of the Jiang Family Manor. In recent years, we have received many cultural relic researchers, amateurs and photographers, all of whom hope to have a book comprehensively introduce the Jiang Family Manor. In the long time of the researches on the Jiang Family Manor, I deeply understand the cultural connotations of this domestic architecture, and have the idea of compiling the valuable materials about it into a book. Under the concern, encouragement and support of the colleagues and friends, I have the strong self-confidence of compiling an album to introduce the Jiang Family Manor.

In May 2006, I started the collection and compilation of the relevant materials. Through years of surveys, examinations and researches, in October 2015, the first sketch of this album was finished; then, by many times of revision, collation, amendment and reselection of materials, I tried my best to thoroughly exhibit the aesthetic values and cultural connotations of the Jiang Family Manor, a rare case of domestic architecture.

At the publishing of this album, I would like to express my grateful thanks to the leaders, colleagues and friends who have made great efforts to the compiling and publishing of this

了 500 余幅图片。2015 年孟冬，画册初稿清样成形。在编纂过程中，"去伪存真、去粗取精"，对姜氏家族世系、人文历史、创业发家、建筑特点、典故传说等资料几易其稿，印证核对，使其具有史实性、观赏性和研究性。为确保质量，又先后对清样进行了多次修改，校正补缺，好中选优。在条目编排、版面设计、视觉观赏等诸方面，力图体现简洁明快、图文并茂，较全面地展现姜氏庄园这一民居瑰宝的价值魅力与文化内涵。

在画册付梓之际，我由衷地感谢为本画册的编纂、出版做了大量工作的领导、同仁和朋友；感谢当代著名画家、原中国美术家协会副主席刘文西为画册题名；感谢西安建筑科技大学王军教授、榆林学院郭冰庐教授分别为画册撰写序言；感谢榆林市文物保护研究所乔建军所长对书稿提出的许多宝贵意见和建议，并在百忙之中撰文予以支持；感谢姜氏庄园住户以及刘家峁村的父老乡亲多年来对我们工作的支持与厚爱。同时，感谢榆林市财政局卢林局长、米脂县财政局胡锦涛局长的鼎力帮助与支持。

因水平所限，难免存在疏误之处，敬请广大读者不吝赐教。

艾克生

2016 年 5 月 16 日

于姜氏庄园文物管理所

album; to Mr. Liu Wenxi, the famous contemporary painter and the former vice-chairman of China Artists Association, who wrote the title for this album; to Professor Wang Jun of Xi'an University of Architecture and Technology and Professor Guo Binglu of Yulin University, who wrote prefaces for the album; to Mr. Qiao Jianjun, the director of Yulin Municipal Institute of Cultural Heritage Conservation, who presented many valuable suggestions and advices for the text, and composed an article to support my job in his busy schedule; to the present residents of the Jiang Family Manor and the fellow villagers of Liujiamao Village, who gave us care and support for our work. Meanwhile, I would like express my gratefulness to Mr. Lu Lin, the director of Yulin Municipal Bureau of Finance and Mr. Hu Jintao, the director of Mizhi County Bureau of Finance, who have given us great helps.

Limited by my knowledge, the careless omissions and mistakes I made in this album are waiting for the instruction and correcting of the readers.

Ai Kesheng

May 16, 2016

At Commission for Preservation

of the Jiang Family Manor